Ninja Creami Recipe Book

1000 Days Ninja Creami Cookbook with Simple and Easy

Recipes for Beginners to Master Your Ice Creami Maker

Heather B. Johnson

Table of content

INTRODUCTION

INTRODUCTION

Preparing healthy and creamy ice creams at home is everyone's dream. But we know how the whole process is difficult to deal with-Having an ice cream maker sure helps! The Ninja CREAMi Ice Cream maker is one such appliance that help you churn all sorts of ice cream, sorbet or smoothies ingredients together. So to help you make all sorts of delicious freezer treats, in this cookbook we bring you the best of the Ninja CREAMi recipe collection. Let's find out!

About Ninja CREAMi Appliance:

Ninja CREAMi is an electric ice cream maker. It is used to make various frozen items like smoothie bowls, milkshakes, sorbet, and ice cream. This is not a blender but rather an appliance that uses "creamify" technology to transform frozen items into ice cream desserts.

The Ninja CREAMi does one of two things instead of equally blending all contents like a blender. To begin, place all of the ingredients in the Ninja CREAMi and process. Using this method, which is comparable to using a blender, all of the components will be evenly combined. If you process chocolate chips, for example, the chocolate chips will all be chopped up into extremely little pieces and dispersed throughout the mixture.

If you want full chocolate chips in your ice cream, you should add them during the mixing process. The mix-ins are "folded" into the base during this step. If you blended everything together, you wouldn't get entire chocolate chips at the end.

Benefits of the Appliance:

This Creami Ninja ice cream machine is easy to use and requires no setup. There are three pint-sized plastic tubs included with the unit. You may make whatever type of frozen dessert you desire in each tub, including sorbets (fruit, sugar, and water), gelato, and ice cream, which can be full-fat, low-fat, or dairy-free. This machine can also create smoothies and milkshakes.

You can only make one flavor of ice cream at a time using a normal ice cream maker. But in Ninja CREAMi you can prepare the base separately and freeze it in pint containers, the Ninja CREAMi allows you to produce as many flavors as you'd like. Simply combine the frozen dessert and add your desired mix-ins when ready to enjoy.

You must freeze your pint-sized tubs of ice cream mix for 20 to 24 hours after whisking up a recipe in a big bowl which should take no more than a few minutes. Once the mix is completely frozen, place it in an outer bowl, cover it with the paddle lid, and load it into the machine. Finally, select the preset for the type of dessert you're preparing, and you'll have a pint of freshly churned ice cream, sorbet, or gelato in less than three minutes.

Features of the appliance:

1. The power button is used to turn on and off the unit.

2. **Install Light**: When the equipment is not properly assembled for use, the install light will illuminate. Make sure the bowl is correctly inserted if the light is blinking. Check that the paddle is installed if the light is solid.

3. **Progress Bar**: It shows how far the One-Touch Program has progressed. When the program is finished, all four progress bar LEDs will blink twice and then switch off.

4. **One-Touch Program**: this program is cleverly designed to prepare delicious items in 1-2 ½ minutes. The length and speed of the program vary based on the best settings for getting flawlessly creamy results for that particular recipe.

   Ice cream: Assembled for dishes that are traditionally rich and decadent. Great for making thick, creamy, scoop-able ice creams from dairy and dairy-alternative recipes.

   Lite Ice Cream: this is designed for people who are health conscious and like to make ice cream with low fats and sugar. When processing keto or paleo, recipes can be chosen.

   Gelato: Mainly designed for Italian-style ice cream with a custard base. When specified, use GELATO to make delectable, delicious desserts.

   Sorbet: It is used to transform fruits that contain sugar and water into creamy delights.

   Smoothie Bowl: Designed for fruit (fresh or frozen) and/or vegetable (frozen) dishes that include dairy, dairy alternatives, or juice.

   Milk Shake: Created to make thick, fast milkshakes. Simply pick MILKSHAKE and blend your favourite ice cream (store-bought or homemade), milk, and mix-ins.

5. **Mix-In**: It is created to fold in pieces of candies, cookies, nuts, cereal, or frozen fruit to prepare a just-processed foundation or store-bought treat.

6. **Re-Spin**: After executing one of the preset programs, this is designed to provide a smooth texture. When the base is very cold (below -7°F), and the texture is brittle rather than creamy, a RE-SPIN is frequently required.

Parts of Creami Ninja Appliance:

There are six parts of this accessory:
- Motor base
- Outer Bowl Lid
- Creamerizer Paddle
- CREAMi Pint Lid
- 16 ounces CREAMi Pint
- Outer Bowl

How to use the Ninja CREAMi Appliance:

To start with, it is important to read the guidebook of the Ninja machine provided with it as it will guide about warnings before starting using it. Some tips for using Creami Ninja Appliance are:

1. Fill the CREAMi Pint with the ingredients. Do not put ingredients past the pint's MAX FILL line. As this machine is not a blender therefore solid block or ice can not be processed in it. Frozen fruit or any other processed hard ingredients can not be added to make a smoothie; all fruits should be crushed before processing.

2. If the ingredients must be frozen for the recipe, snap the lid on the pint and place it in the freezer for at least 24 hours. When freezing, some points to ponder are Make sure your freezer's temperature is adjusted correctly if it's changeable. The equipment can handle bases with a temperature range of 9°F to -7°F. Your pint should reach the proper temperature if your freezer is within this range. The base has to freeze for at least 24 hours before it can be processed. Do not freeze the pint at an angle to avoid harming your machine. Place the pint in the freezer on a level surface.

3. Place the device on a clean, dry, level surface, such as a countertop or table, and plug it in.

4. Remove the pint lid and set the pint in the outer bowl once the base is ready or frozen. Before refreezing in the pint, always smooth up the surface of a prepared dessert. Put the pint in the fridge to allow the components to melt if the pint is frozen unevenly. Then whisk to ensure that all of the ingredients are well blended. Refreeze the pint, making sure it's on a level surface in the

freezer.

5. Insert the Creamerizer Paddle in the bottom of the outer bowl cover by pressing and holding the paddle clasp on the top of the lid. To secure the paddle, release the lock. The lock will be fixed, and the paddle will be slightly loose when fully attached.

6. Place the lid's tab just to the right of the outer bowl handle, aligning the lines on the lid and handle. To lock the lid, turn it clockwise.

7. Check to see if the unit is connected. Then, with the handle positioned below the control panel, place the outer bowl onto the motor base. To lift the platform and lock the bowl in position, twist the handle to the right. When the bowl is entirely inserted, you will hear a click.

8. To turn on the unit, press the power button. The One-Touch Programs will display, and the machine will be ready to use if the outer bowl is correctly inserted. Choose the program that is most appropriate for your recipe. When the function is finished, it will shut off automatically.

9. When the program is finished, remove the outer bowl by twisting the handle back to the centre while holding the bowl release button on the left side of the motor base. The platform lowers the bowl as the handle is turned. To remove the bowl, lift it.

10. The lid unlocks button is pressed, and the lid is twisted counterclockwise to remove the lid.

11. Use a spoon to make one 1/2-inch wide hole in the bottom of the pint if adding mix-ins. To process again with the MIX-IN programs, add chopped or broken mix-ins to the hole in the pint and repeat steps 6-10.

12. If you don't want to add mix-ins, RE-SPIN can be used to make a crumbly or powdered pint to make it creamier. For very cold bases, RE-SPIN is frequently required. Suppose the dessert is smooth and scoopable; lift the pint out of the outer bowl. If the base is crumbly or powdery, repeat steps 6–10 with the RE-SPIN program to process it again.

Care and Maintenance:

1. ***Cleaning***: Remove the Creamerizer Paddle from the outer bowl lid by cleaning the lid and then pushing the paddle latch before cleaning.

2. ***Hand-Washing***: In warm, soapy water, wash the containers, lids, and paddle. To clean the paddle, use a dishwashing utensil with a handle. Rinse and air-dry all portions thoroughly.

3. ***Dishwasher:*** Before putting the paddle, pint, outer bowl, and lids in the dishwasher, make sure they're all separated.

4. ***Outer Bowl Lid:*** for cleaning the outer bowl lid, remove the paddle because ingredients may get stuck to the paddle. Then wash it thoroughly with warm and soapy water with hands.

5. ***Motor Base***: Before cleaning, unplug the motor base. Clean the motor base with a moist cloth. To clean the base, do not use abrasive rags, pads, or brushes. After each use, wipe the spindle beneath the control panel with a moist cloth.

6. ***Storing***: Wrap the cable with the hook-and-loop fastener near the back of the motor base for cold storage. For storage, do not wrap the cable over the bottom of the base. Any remaining attachments should be stored next to the device or in a cabinet where they won't be destroyed.

7. ***Resetting the Motor***: This unit has a unique safety system that protects the motor and drive system from damage if it is accidentally overloaded. The motor will be momentarily disabled if the unit is overloaded. If this happens, take the steps outlined below to reset the device:

   - Disconnect the machine from the power source.
   - Set aside for 15 minutes to allow the unit to cool.
   - Take the outer bowl lid off and the paddle with it.
   - Make sure the lid assembly isn't clogged with ingredients.

Chapter 1 Smoothie Bowls Recipes

Chapter 1 Smoothie Bowls Recipes

Chocolate Fudge Frosting

Prep time: 5 minutes | Cook time: 5 minutes | Serves 1
½ cup cold unsalted butter, cut in 8 pieces
1½ cups confectioners' sugar
2 tablespoons dark unsweetened cocoa powder
1 tablespoon heavy (whipping) cream
1 teaspoon vanilla extract

1. Place all the ingredients in a clean CREAMi Pint in the order listed. 2. Place the pint in the outer bowl of your Ninja CREAMi, install the Creamerizer Paddle in the outer bowl lid, and lock the lid assembly onto the outer bowl. Place the bowl assembly on the motor base, and twist the handle to the right to raise the platform and lock it in place. Select the Re-Spin function. 3. Once the machine has finished processing, the frosting should be smooth and easily scoopable with a spoon. If the frosting is too thick, select the Re-Spin function again and process until creamy and smooth.

Oat Banana Smoothie Bowl

Prep time: 5 minutes | Cook time: 1 minutes | Serves 2
½ cup water
¼ cup quick oats
1 cup vanilla Greek yogurt
½ cup banana, peeled and sliced
3 tablespoons honey

1. In a small microwave-safe bowl, add the water and oats and microwave on High or about one minute. 2. Remove from the microwave and stir in the yogurt, banana and honey until well combined. 3. Transfer the mixture into an empty Ninja CREAMi pint container. 4. Cover the container with storage lid and freeze for 24 hours. 5. After 24 hours, remove the lid from container and arrange into the Outer Bowl of Ninja CREAMi. 6. Install the Creamerizer Paddle onto the lid of Outer Bowl. 7. Then rotate the lid clockwise to lock. 8. Press Power button to turn on the unit. 9. Then press Smoothie Bowl button. 10. When the program is completed, turn the Outer Bowl and release it from the machine. 11. Transfer the smoothie into

serving bowls and serve with your favorite topping.

Coffee Smoothie Bowl

Prep time: 5 minutes | Cook time: 3 minutes | Serves 2
2 cups unsweetened vanilla almond milk
¼ cup instant coffee

1. In a large bowl, add the almond milk and instant coffee mix and beat until well combine 2. Transfer the mixture into an empty Ninja CREAMi pint container. 3. Cover the container with storage lid and freeze for 24 hours. 4. After 24 hours, remove the lid from container and arrange into the Outer Bowl of Ninja CREAMi. 5. Install the Creamerizer Paddle onto the lid of Outer Bowl. 6. Then rotate the lid clockwise to lock. 7. Press Power button to turn on the unit. 8. Then press Smoothie Bowl button. 9. When the program is completed, turn the Outer Bowl and release it from the machine. 10. Transfer the smoothie into serving bowls and serve immediately.

Fruity Coffee Smoothie Bowl

Prep time: 5 minutes | Cook time: 3 minutes | Serves 4
1 cup brewed coffee
½ cup oat milk
2 tablespoons almond butter
1 cup fresh raspberries
1 large banana, peeled and sliced

1. In a high-speed blender add all the ingredients and pulse until smooth. 2. Transfer the mixture into an empty Ninja CREAMi pint container. 3. Cover the container with the storage lid and freeze for 24 hours. 4. After 24 hours, remove the lid from container and arrange into the outer bowl of Ninja CREAMi. 5. Install the "Creamerizer Paddle" onto the lid of outer bowl. 6. Then rotate the lid clockwise to lock. 7. Press "Power" button to turn on the unit. 8. Then press "SMOOTHIE BOWL" button. 9. When the program is completed, turn the outer bowl and release it from the machine. 10. Transfer the smoothie into serving bowls and serve immediately.

Avocado & Banana Smoothie Bowl

Prep time: 5 minutes | Cook time: 5 minutes | Serves 4

½ cup unsweetened coconut milk
¼ cup fresh apple juice
2 tablespoons whey protein isolate
4-5 tablespoons maple syrup
¼ teaspoon vanilla extract
1 cup ripe avocado, peeled, pitted and cut in ½-inch pieces
1 cup fresh banana, peeled and cut in ½-inch pieces

1. In a large bowl, add the coconut milk, apple juice, protein isolate, maple syrup and vanilla extract and beat until well combined. 2. Place the avocado and banana into an empty Ninja CREAMi pint container and with the back of a spoon, firmly press the fruit below the MAX FILL line. 3. Top with coconut milk mixture and mix until well combined. 4. Cover the container with the storage lid and freeze for 24 hours. 5. After 24 hours, remove the lid from container and arrange into the outer bowl of Ninja CREAMi. 6. Install the "Creamerizer Paddle" onto the lid of outer bowl. 7. Then rotate the lid clockwise to lock. 8. Press "Power" button to turn on the unit. 9. Then press "SMOOTHIE BOWL" button. 10. When the program is completed, turn the outer bowl and release it from the machine. 11. Transfer the smoothie into serving bowls and serve immediately.

Raspberry & Orange Smoothie Bowl

Prep time: 5 minutes | Cook time: 5 minutes | Serves 2

2 cups fresh raspberries
½ cup vanilla yogurt
¼ cup fresh orange juice
1 tablespoon honey

1. In an empty Ninja CREAMi pint container, place the raspberries and with the back of a spoon, firmly press the berries below the MAX FILL line. 2. Add the yogurt, orange juice and honey and stir to combine. 3. Cover the container with the storage lid and freeze for 24 hours. 4. After 24 hours, remove the lid from container and arrange into the outer bowl of Ninja CREAMi. 5. Install the "Creamerizer Paddle" onto the lid of outer bowl. 6. Then rotate the lid clockwise to lock. 7. Press "Power" button to turn on the unit. 8. Then press "SMOOTHIE BOWL" button. 9. When the program is completed, turn the outer bowl and release it from the machine. 10. Transfer the smoothie into serving bowls and serve immediately.

Buttery Coffee Smoothie

Prep time: 5 minutes | Cook time: 5 minutes | Serves 1
1 cup brewed coffee
2 large pasteurized egg yolks
¼ cup avocado
¼ cup ice cubes
1 tablespoon coconut sugar
2 tablespoons coconut oil, melted

1. Combine the coffee, egg yolks, avocado, ice cubes, and coconut sugar in an empty ninja CREAMi Pint. 2. Place the Ninja CREAMi Pint into the outer bowl. Place the outer bowl with the Pint in it into the ninja CREAMi machine and turn until the outer bowl locks into place. Push the SMOOTHIE button. During the SMOOTHIE function, the ingredients will mix together and become very creamy. 3. Once the SMOOTHIE function has ended, turn the outer bowl and release it from the ninja CREAMi machine. 4. Scoop the smoothie into a tall glass.

Kale, Avocado & Fruit Smoothie Bowl

Prep time: 5 minutes | Cook time: 3 minutes | Serves 4
1 banana, peeled and cut into 1-inch pieces
½ of avocado, peeled, pitted and cut into 1-inch pieces
1 cup fresh kale leaves
1 cup green apple, peeled, cored and cut into 1-inch pieces
¼ cup unsweetened coconut milk
2 tablespoons agave nectar

1. In a large high-speed blender, add all the ingredients and pulse until smooth. 2. Transfer the mixture into an empty Ninja CREAMi pint container. 3. Cover the container with storage lid and freeze for 24 hours. 4. After 24 hours, remove the lid from container and arrange into the Outer Bowl of Ninja CREAMi. 5. Install the Creamerizer Paddle onto the lid of Outer Bowl. 6. Then rotate the lid clockwise to lock. 7. Press Power button to turn on the unit. 8. Then press Smoothie Bowl button. 9. When the program is completed, turn the Outer Bowl and release it from the machine. 10. Transfer the smoothie into serving bowls and serve immediately.

Microwave Vanilla Cake

Prep time: 5 minutes | Cook time: 5 minutes | Serves 2
½ teaspoon vanilla extract
3 tablespoons whole milk
2 tablespoons unsalted butter
⅛ teaspoon kosher salt
½ teaspoon baking powder
2 tablespoons granulated sugar
¼ cup all-purpose flour
Chocolate Fudge Frosting, for serving (optional)

1. Place all the ingredients except for the frosting in a clean CREAMi Pint container in the order listed. 2. Place the pint in the outer bowl of your Ninja CREAMi, install the Creamerizer Paddle in the outer bowl lid, and lock the lid assembly onto the outer bowl. Place the bowl assembly on the motor base, and twist the handle to the right to raise the platform and lock it in place. Select the Re-Spin function. 3. Once the machine has finished processing, place the pint container in the microwave and cook on High for 2 minutes. Check the cake for doneness—a skewer or knife inserted into the cake should come out clean, and the cake should pull away from the sides of the pint container. 4. Once the container is cool enough to handle, run a butter knife around the inside of the pint. Flip the pint over, and the cake should pop right out. 5. If you want to add frosting, slice the cake widthwise into 3 layers. Place one slice on a plate and frost the top of the layer. Lay a second slice on top of the first and frost the top. Top with the final slice of cake, then frost the top and sides of the assembled cake. 6. Cut in half and serve.

Fruity Coconut Smoothie Bowl

Prep time: 5 minutes | Cook time: 5 minutes | Serves 2
½ of ripe banana, peeled and cut in ½-inch pieces
¼ cup coconut rum
¼ cup unsweetened coconut cream
½ cup unsweetened canned coconut milk
¾ cup pineapple juice
2 tablespoons fresh lime juice

1. In a large bowl, add all the ingredients and beat until well combined. 2. Transfer the mixture into an empty Ninja CREAMi pint container. 3. Cover the container with the storage lid and freeze for 24 hours. 4. After 24 hours, remove the lid from

container and arrange into the outer bowl of Ninja CREAMi. 5. Install the "Creamerizer Paddle" onto the lid of outer bowl. 6. Then rotate the lid clockwise to lock. 7. Press "Power" button to turn on the unit. 8. Then press "SMOOTHIE BOWL" button. 9. When the program is completed, turn the outer bowl and release it from the machine. 10. Transfer the smoothie into serving bowl sand serve immediately.

Pumpkin & Banana Smoothie Bowl

Prep time: 5 minutes | Cook time: 3 minutes | Serves 2
1 cup canned pumpkin puree
⅓ cup plain Greek yogurt
1½ tablespoons maple syrup
1 teaspoon vanilla extract
1 teaspoon pumpkin pie spice
1 frozen banana, peeled and cut in ½-inch pieces

1. In an empty Ninja CREAMi pint container, add the pumpkin puree, yogurt, maple syrup, vanilla extract, and pumpkin pie spice and mix well. 2. Add the banana pieces and stir to combine. 3. Transfer the mixture into an empty Ninja CREAMi pint container. 4. Arrange the container into the outer bowl of Ninja CREAMi. 5. Install the "Creamerizer Paddle" onto the lid of outer bowl. 6. Then rotate the lid clockwise to lock. 7. Press "Power" button to turn on the unit. 8. Then press "SMOOTHIE BOWL" button. 9. When the program is completed, turn the outer bowl and release it from the machine. 10. Transfer the smoothie into serving bowls and serve immediately.

Gator Smoothies

Prep time: 5 minutes | Cook time: 5 minutes | Serves 1
1 cup ice
1 cup grape-flavored sports drink
1 scoop vanilla ice cream

1. Add the ice, sports drink, and ice cream into an empty ninja CREAMi Pint. 2. Place the Ninja CREAMi Pint into the outer bowl. Place the outer bowl with the Pint in it into the ninja CREAMi machine and turn until the outer bowl locks into place. Push the SMOOTHIE button. During the SMOOTHIE function, the ingredients will mix together and become very creamy. 3. Once the SMOOTHIE function has ended, turn the outer bowl and release it from the ninja CREAMi

machine. 4. Pour into a tall glass.

Pineapple Smoothie Bowl

Prep time: 5 minutes | Cook time: 5 minutes | Serves 4
2 ripe bananas, peeled and cut in 1-inch pieces
1 cup fresh pineapple, chopped
¼ cup yogurt
2 tablespoons honey

1. In a large bowl, add all the ingredients and beat until well combined. 2. Transfer the mixture into an empty Ninja CREAMi pint container. 3. Cover the container with storage lid and freeze for 24 hours. 4. After 24 hours, remove the lid from container and arrange into the Outer Bowl of Ninja CREAMi. 5. Install the Creamerizer Paddle onto the lid of Outer Bowl. 6. Then rotate the lid clockwise to lock. 7. Press Power button to turn on the unit. 8. Then press Smoothie Bowl button. 9. When the program is completed, turn the Outer Bowl and release it from the machine. 10. Transfer the smoothie into serving bowls and serve immediately.

Frozen Fruit Smoothie Bowl

Prep time: 5 minutes | Cook time: 3 minutes | Serves 2
1 ripe banana, peeled and cut in 1-inch pieces
2 cups frozen fruit mix
1¼ cups vanilla yogurt

1. In a large high-speed blender, add all the ingredients and pulse until smooth. 2. Transfer the mixture into an empty Ninja CREAMi pint container. 3. Cover the container with the storage lid and freeze for 24 hours. 4. After 24 hours, remove the lid from container and arrange into the outer bowl of Ninja CREAMi. 5. Install the "Creamerizer Paddle" onto the lid of outer bowl. 6. Then rotate the lid clockwise to lock. 7. Press "Power" button to turn on the unit. 8. Then press "SMOOTHIE BOWL" button. 9. When the program is completed, turn the outer bowl and release it from the machine. 10. Transfer the smoothie into serving bowls and serve immediately.

Chocolate Pumpkin Smoothie Bowl

Prep time: 5 minutes | Cook time: 3 minutes | Serves 4
½ cup canned pumpkin puree
2 tablespoons unsweetened cocoa powder
1 teaspoon pumpkin spice seasoning
2 ripe bananas, cut in ½-inch pieces
1 tablespoon agave nectar
¼ cup whole milk

1. In a small bowl, stir together the pumpkin puree, cocoa powder, and pumpkin spice until well combined. Pour the base into a clean CREAMi Pint. Mix in the bananas, agave, and milk until everything is fully combined and the bananas are coated. Place the storage lid on the container and freeze for 24 hours. 2. Remove the pint from the freezer and take off the lid. Place the pint in the outer bowl of your Ninja CREAMi, install the Creamerizer Paddle in the outer bowl lid, and lock the lid assembly onto the outer bowl. Place the bowl assembly on the motor base, and twist the handle to the right to raise the platform and lock it in place. Select the Smoothie Bowl function. 3. Once the machine has finished processing, remove the smoothie bowl from the pint. Serve immediately with your desired toppings.

Papaya Smoothie Bowl

Prep time: 5 minutes | Cook time: 3 minutes | Serves 2
2 cups ripe papaya, peeled and cut into 1-inch pieces
14 ounces (397 g) whole milk
4-6 drops liquid stevia
¼ teaspoon vanilla extract

1. Place the mango pieces into an empty Ninja CREAMi pint container. 2. Top with coconut milk, stevia and vanilla extract and stir to combine. 3. Cover the container with the storage lid and freeze for 24 hours. 4. After 24 hours, remove the lid from container and arrange into the outer bowl of Ninja CREAMi. 5. Install the "Creamerizer Paddle" onto the lid of outer bowl. 6. Then rotate the lid clockwise to lock. 7. Press "Power" button to turn on the unit. 8. Then press "SMOOTHIE BOWL" button. 9. When the program is completed, turn the outer bowl and release it from the machine. 10. Transfer the smoothie into serving bowls and serve immediately.

Chocolate, Peanut Butter & Banana Smoothie

Prep time: 5 minutes | Cook time: 5 minutes | Serves 2
1 cup chocolate pudding
1 tablespoon creamy peanut butter
1 large ripe banana, cut into pieces
⅔ cup reduced-fat milk
½ cup ice cubes
Reddi-wip chocolate dairy whipped topping

1. Mash the bananas in a large bowl and add all the other ingredients except for the whipped topping. Combine and put into the ninja CREAMi Pint. 2. Place the Pint into the outer bowl. Place the outer bowl with the Pint in it into the ninja CREAMi machine and turn until the outer bowl locks into place. Push the SMOOTHIE button. The ingredients will mix together and become very creamy. 3. Once the SMOOTHIE function has ended, turn the outer bowl and release it from the ninja CREAMi machine. 4. Scoop the smoothie into glass bowls to serve.

Simple Smoothie Bowl

Prep time: 5 minutes | Cook time: 5 minutes | Serves 2
1 bottle fruit smoothie beverage

1. Pour the smoothie beverage into a clean CREAMi Pint. Place the storage lid on the container and freeze for 24 hours 2. Remove the pint from the freezer and take off the lid. Place the pint in the outer bowl of your Ninja CREAMi, install the Creamerizer Paddle in the outer bowl lid, and lock the lid assembly onto the outer bowl. Place the bowl assembly on the motor base, and twist the handle to the right to raise the platform and lock it in place. Select the Smoothie Bowl function. 3. Once the machine has finished processing, remove the smoothie bowl from the pint. Serve immediately with desired toppings.

Strawberry Smoothie Bowl

Prep time: 5 minutes | Cook time: 5 minutes | Serves 4
2 tablespoons vanilla protein powder
¼ cup agave nectar
¼ cup pineapple juice
½ cup whole milk
1 cup ripe banana, peeled and cut in ½-inch pieces

1 cup fresh strawberries, hulled and quartered

1. In a large bowl, add the protein powder, agave nectar, pineapple juice and milk and beat until well combined. 2. Place the banana and strawberry into an empty Ninja CREAMi pint container and with the back of a spoon, firmly press the fruit below the Max Fill line. 3. Top with milk mixture and mix until well combined. 4. Cover the container with storage lid and freeze for 24 hours. 5. After 24 hours, remove the lid from container and arrange into the Outer Bowl of Ninja CREAMi. 6. Install the Creamerizer Paddle onto the lid of Outer Bowl. 7. Then rotate the lid clockwise to lock. 8. Press Power button to turn on the unit. 9. Then press Smoothie Bowl button. 10. When the program is completed, turn the Outer Bowl and release it from the machine. 11. Transfer the smoothie into serving bowls and serve immediately.

Energy Elixir Smoothie

Prep time: 5 minutes | Cook time: 5 minutes | Serves 1
½ cup spring salad greens
½ cup frozen red grapes
½ chopped frozen banana
½ cored and chopped frozen pear
2 tablespoons walnuts
Water as needed

1. Layer the salad greens, red grapes, banana, pear, walnuts, and enough water to cover the mixture in an empty ninja CREAMi Pint. 2. Place the Ninja CREAMi Pint into the outer bowl. Place the outer bowl with the Pint in it into the ninja CREAMi machine and turn until the outer bowl locks into place. Push the SMOOTHIE button. During the SMOOTHIE function, the ingredients will mix together and become very creamy. 3. Once the SMOOTHIE function has ended, turn the outer bowl and release it from the ninja CREAMi machine. 4. Scoop the smoothie into a glass.

Chapter 2 Sorbet Recipes

Chapter 2 Sorbet Recipes

Acai & Fruit Sorbet

Prep time: 5 minutes | Cook time: 5 minutes | Serves 4
1 packet frozen acai
½ cup blackberries
½ cup banana, peeled and sliced
¼ cup granulated sugar
1 cup water

1. In a high-speed blender, add all the ingredients and pulse until smooth. 2. Transfer the mixture into an empty Ninja CREAMi pint container. 3. Cover the container with storage lid and freeze for 24 hours. 4. After 24 hours, remove the lid from container and arrange into the Outer Bowl of Ninja CREAMi. 5. Install the Creamerizer Paddle onto the lid of Outer Bowl. 6. Then rotate the lid clockwise to lock. 7. Press Power button to turn on the unit. 8. Then press Sorbet button. 9. When the program is completed, turn the Outer Bowl and release it from the machine. 10. Transfer the sorbet into serving bowls and serve immediately.

Cherry-berry Rosé Sorbet

Prep time: 5 minutes | Cook time: 10 minutes | Serves 3
2 cups frozen cherry-berry fruit blend
½ cup rosé wine, or as needed
¼ cup white sugar, or to taste
¼ medium lemon, juiced

1. Add all ingredients to a bowl and mix until the sugar dissolves. Place the mixture in the ninja CREAMi Pint container and freeze on a level surface in a cold freezer for a full 24 hours. 2. After 24 hours, remove the Pint from the freezer. Remove the lid. 3. Place the Ninja CREAMi Pint into the outer bowl. Place the outer bowl with the Pint in it into the ninja CREAMi machine and turn until the outer bowl locks into place. Push the SORBET button. During the SORBET function, the sorbet will mix together and become very creamy. This should take approximately 2 minutes. 4. Once the SORBET function has ended, turn the outer bowl and release it from the ninja CREAMi machine. 5. Your sorbet is ready to eat! Enjoy!

Blueberry Lemon Sorbet

Prep time: 5 minutes | Cook time: 5 minutes | Serves 1

1 tablespoon cream cheese

¼ cup milk

1½ cups lemonade

⅓ cup blueberries (fresh or frozen)

1. In a medium mixing bowl, whisk together the softened cream cheese and the milk. Make an effort to integrate the two as much as possible. Some little bits of cream cheese may remain, but that's fine as long as they're small. 2. Add the lemonade and stir thoroughly. 3. Pour the mixture into a ninja CREAMi Pint container, add the blueberries and freeze on a level surface in a cold freezer for a full 24 hours. 4. After 24 hours, remove the Pint from the freezer. Remove the lid. 5. Place the Ninja CREAMi Pint into the outer bowl. Place the outer bowl with the Pint in it into the ninja CREAMi machine and turn until the outer bowl locks into place. Push the SORBET button. During the SORBET function, the sorbet will mix together and become very creamy. This should take approximately 2 minutes. 6. Once the SORBET function has ended, turn the outer bowl and release it from the ninja CREAMi machine. 7. Your sorbet is ready to eat! Enjoy! 8. Place the outer bowl with the Pint back into the ninja CREAMi machine and lock it into place if the sorbet isn't quite creamy enough. Select the RE-SPIN option. Remove the outer bowl from the Ninja CREAMi after the RE-SPIN cycle is complete.

Lemony Herb Sorbet

Prep time: 5 minutes | Cook time: 6 minutes | Serves 4

½ cup water

¼ cup granulated sugar

2 large fresh dill sprigs, stemmed

2 large fresh basil sprigs, stemmed

1 cup ice water

2 tablespoons fresh lemon juice

1. In a small saucepan, add sugar and water and over medium heat and cook for about five minutes or until the sugar is dissolved, stirring continuously. 2. Stir in the herb sprigs and remove from the heat. 3. Add the ice water and lemon juice and stir to combine. 4. Transfer the mixture into an empty Ninja CREAMi pint container. 5. Cover the container with storage lid and freeze for 24 hours. 6. After 24 hours, remove the lid from container and arrange into the Outer Bowl of Ninja

CREAMi. 7. Install the Creamerizer Paddle onto the lid of Outer Bowl. 8. Then rotate the lid clockwise to lock. 9. Press Power button to turn on the unit. 10. Then press Sorbet button. 11. When the program is completed, turn the Outer Bowl and release it from the machine. 12. Transfer the sorbet into serving bowls and serve immediately.

Italian Ice Sorbet

Prep time: 5 minutes | Cook time: 5 minutes | Serves 1
12 ounces lemonade
Sugar or your preferred sweetener to taste (optional)
If the lemonade you're using is quite tart, use 6 ounces of lemonade and 6 ounces of water instead of 12 ounces of lemonade

1. Pour the lemonade (or lemonade and water mixture) into a ninja CREAMi Pint container and freeze on a level surface in a cold freezer for a full 24 hours. 2. After 24 hours, remove the Pint from the freezer. Remove the lid. 3. Place the Ninja CREAMi Pint into the outer bowl. Place the outer bowl with the Pint in it into the ninja CREAMi machine and turn until the outer bowl locks into place. Push the SORBET button. During the SORBET function, the sorbet will mix together and become very creamy. This should take approximately 2 minutes. 4. Once the SORBET function has ended, turn the outer bowl and release it from the ninja CREAMi machine.

Strawberry & Beet Sorbet

Prep time: 5 minutes | Cook time: 5 minutes | Serves 4
2⅔ cups strawberries, hulled and quartered
⅓ cup cooked beets, quartered
⅓ cup granulated sugar
⅓ cup orange juice

1. In a high-speed blender, add mangoes and beets and pulse until smooth. 2. Through a fine-mesh strainer, strain the mango puree into a large bowl. 3. Add the sugar and orange juice and and stir to combine. 4. Transfer the mixture into an empty Ninja CREAMi pint container. 5. Cover the container with the storage lid and freeze for 24 hours. 6. After 24 hours, remove the lid from container and arrange into the outer bowl of Ninja CREAMi. 7. Install the "Creamerizer Paddle" onto the lid of outer bowl. 8. Then rotate the lid clockwise to lock. 9. Press "Power" button to turn on the unit. 10. Then press "SORBET" button. 11. When the program

is completed, turn the outer bowl and release it from the machine. 12. Transfer the sorbet into serving bowls and serve immediately.

Pear Sorbet

Prep time: 5 minutes | Cook time: 5 minutes | Serves 4
1 can pears in light syrup

1. Place the pear pieces into an empty Ninja CREAMi to the MAX FILL line. 2. Cover the orange pieces with syrup from the can. 3. Cover the container with the storage lid and freeze for 24 hours. 4. After 24 hours, remove the lid from container and arrange into the outer bowl of Ninja CREAMi. 5. Install the "Creamerizer Paddle" onto the lid of outer bowl. 6. Then rotate the lid clockwise to lock. 7. Press "Power" button to turn on the unit. 8. Then press "SORBET" button. 9. When the program is completed, turn the outer bowl and release it from the machine. 10. Transfer the sorbet into serving bowls and serve immediately.

Mango Margarita Sorbet

Prep time: 5 minutes | Cook time: 5 minutes | Serves 4
¾ cup margarita mix
3 tablespoons gold tequila
2 tablespoons fresh lime juice
1 tablespoon agave nectar
¼ teaspoon cayenne pepper
¼ teaspoon salt
1 can mango chunks

1. In a bowl, add all ingredients except for mango chunks and beat until well combined. 2. Add mango chunks and toss to coat. 3. Transfer the mixture into an empty Ninja CREAMi pint container. 4. Cover the container with the storage lid and freeze for 24 hours. 5. After 24 hours, remove the lid from container and arrange into the outer bowl of Ninja CREAMi. 6. Install the "Creamerizer Paddle" onto the lid of outer bowl. 7. Then rotate the lid clockwise to lock. 8. Press "Power" button to turn on the unit. 9. Then press "SORBET" button. 10. When the program is completed, turn the outer bowl and release it from the machine. 11. Transfer the sorbet into serving bowls and serve immediately.

Raspberry Lime Sorbet

Prep time: 5 minutes | Cook time: 5 minutes | Serves 4
2 cups fresh raspberries
5 ounces simple syrup
6 tablespoons fresh lime juice

1. In an empty Ninja CREAMi pint container, add all the ingredients and mix well. 2. Cover the container with the storage lid and freeze for 24 hours. 3. After 24 hours, remove the lid from container and arrange into the outer bowl of Ninja CREAMi. 4. Install the "Creamerizer Paddle" onto the lid of outer bowl. 5. Then rotate the lid clockwise to lock. 6. Press "Power" button to turn on the unit. 7. Then press "SORBET" button. 8. When the program is completed, turn the outer bowl and release it from the machine. 9. Transfer the sorbet into serving bowls and serve immediately.

Mango Sorbet

Prep time: 5 minutes | Cook time: 5 minutes | Serves 4
4 cups mangoes, peeled, pitted and chopped
½ cup water
⅓-½ cup sugar
¼ cup fresh lime juice
2 tablespoons Chamoy

1. In a high-speed blender, add mangoes and water and pulse until smooth. 2. Through a fine-mesh strainer, strain the mango puree into a large bowl. 3. Add the sugar, lime juice and chamoy and stir to combine. 4. Transfer the mixture into an empty Ninja CREAMi pint container. 5. Cover the container with storage lid and freeze for 24 hours. 6. After 24 hours, remove the lid from container and arrange into the Outer Bowl of Ninja CREAMi. 7. Install the Creamerizer Paddle onto the lid of Outer Bowl. 8. Then rotate the lid clockwise to lock. 9. Press Power button to turn on the unit. 10. Then press Sorbet button. 11. When the program is completed, turn the Outer Bowl and release it from the machine. 12. Transfer the sorbet into serving bowls and serve immediately.

Blueberry & Pomegranate Sorbet

Prep time: 5 minutes | Cook time: 5 minutes | Serves 4
1 can blueberries in light syrup
½ cup pomegranate juice

1. In an empty Ninja CREAMi pint container, place the blueberries and top with syrup. 2. Add in the pomegranate juice and stir to combine. 3. Cover the container with the storage lid and freeze for 24 hours. 4. After 24 hours, remove the lid from container and arrange into the outer bowl of Ninja CREAMi. 5. Install the "Creamerizer Paddle" onto the lid of outer bowl. 6. Then rotate the lid clockwise to lock 7. Press "Power" button to turn on the unit. 8. Then press "SORBET" button. 9. When the program is completed, turn the outer bowl and release it from the machine. 10. Transfer the sorbet into serving bowls and serve immediately.

Avocado Lime Sorbet

Prep time: 5 minutes | Cook time: 5 minutes | Serves 4
¾ cup water
2 tablespoons light corn syrup
Pinch of sea salt
⅔ cup granulated sugar
1 large ripe avocado, peeled, pitted and chopped
3 ounces fresh lime juice

1. In a medium saucepan, add water, corn syrup and salt and beat until well combined. 2. Place the saucepan over medium heat. 3. Slowly add the sugar, continuously beating until well combined and bring to a boil. 4. Remove the saucepan from heat and set aside to cool completely. 5. In a high-speed blender, add the sugar mixture, avocado and lime juice and pulse until smooth. 6. Transfer the mixture into an empty Ninja CREAMi pint container. 7. Cover the container with the storage lid and freeze for 24 hours. 8. After 24 hours, remove the lid from container and arrange into the outer bowl of Ninja CREAMi. 9. Install the "Creamerizer Paddle" onto the lid of outer bowl. 10. Then rotate the lid clockwise to lock. 11. Press "Power" button to turn on the unit. 12. Then press "SORBET" button. 13. When the program is completed, turn the outer bowl and release it from the machine. 14. Transfer the sorbet into serving bowls and serve immediately.

Celery Sorbet

Prep time: 5 minutes | Cook time: 5 minutes | Serves 3

½ cup white sugar
½ cup cold water
½ pound trimmed celery
Pinch of salt, or to taste
½ medium lime, juiced

1. In a saucepan over medium heat, combine the sugar and water until it just begins to boil. Remove the pan from the heat. While the other ingredients are being prepared, cool the simple syrup to room temperature. 2. The celery should be cut into tiny pieces. Combine the salt, lime juice, and the cooled simple syrup in a mixing bowl. Blend until completely smooth. 3. Fill a sieve with the mixture. Using a spoon, press the mixture through the strainer until all of the juice has been removed. Cover and refrigerate the juice for at least 1 hour or until completely cooled. 4. Put the cooled mixture into the ninja CREAMi Pint container and freeze on a level surface in a cold freezer for a full 24 hours. 5. After 24 hours, remove the Pint from the freezer. Remove the lid. 6. Place the Ninja CREAMi Pint into the outer bowl. Place the outer bowl with the Pint in it into the ninja CREAMi machine and turn until the outer bowl locks into place. Push the SORBET button. During the SORBET function, the sorbet will mix together and become very creamy. This should take approximately 2 minutes. 7. Once the SORBET function has ended, turn the outer bowl and release it from the ninja CREAMi machine. 8. Your sorbet is ready to eat! Enjoy!

Coconut Lime Sorbet

Prep time: 5 minutes | Cook time: 30 minutes | Serves 5

1 can coconut cream
½ cup coconut water
¼ cup lime juice
½ tablespoon lime zest
¼ teaspoon coconut extract (optional)

1. Combine the coconut cream, coconut water, lime juice, lime zest, and coconut extract in a mixing bowl. Cover with plastic wrap and refrigerate for at least 1 hour, or until the flavors have melded. 2. Add the mixture to the Ninja CREAMi Pint container and freeze on a level surface in a cold freezer for a full 24 hours. 3. After 24 hours, remove the Pint from the freezer. Remove the lid. 4. Place the Ninja

CREAMi Pint into the outer bowl. Place the outer bowl with the Pint in it into the ninja CREAMi machine and turn until the outer bowl locks into place. Push the SORBET button. During the SORBET function, the sorbet will mix together and become very creamy. This should take approximately 2 minutes. 5. Once the SORBET function has ended, turn the outer bowl and release it from the ninja CREAMi machine. 6. Your sorbet is ready to eat! Enjoy!

Peach Sorbet

Prep time: 5 minutes | Cook time: 5 minutes | Serves 4
1 cup passionfruit seltzer
3 tablespoons agave nectar
1 can peaches in heavy syrup, drained

1. In a bowl, add the seltzer and agave and beat until agave is dissolved. 2. Place the peaches into an empty Ninja CREAMi pint container and top with seltzer mixture. 3. Cover the container with storage lid and freeze for 24 hours. 4. After 24 hours, remove the lid from container and arrange into the Outer Bowl of Ninja CREAMi. 5. Install the Creamerizer Paddle onto the lid of Outer Bowl. 6. Then rotate the lid clockwise to lock. 7. Press Power button to turn on the unit. 8. Then press Sorbet button. 9. When the program is completed, turn the Outer Bowl and release it from the machine. 10. Transfer the sorbet into serving bowls and serve immediately.

Lime Beer Sorbet

Prep time: 5 minutes | Cook time: 5 minutes | Serves 4
¾ cup beer
⅔ cup water
½ cup fresh lime juice
¼ cup granulated sugar

1. In a high-speed blender, add all the ingredients and pulse until smooth. 2. Set aside for about 5 minutes. 3. Transfer the mixture into an empty Ninja CREAMi pint container. 4. Cover the container with the storage lid and freeze for 24 hours. 5. After 24 hours, remove the lid from container and arrange into the outer bowl of Ninja CREAMi. 6. Install the "Creamerizer Paddle" onto the lid of outer bowl. 7. Then rotate the lid clockwise to lock. 8. Press "Power" button to turn on the unit. 9. Then press "SORBET" button. 10. When the program is completed, turn the outer bowl and release it from the machine 11. Transfer the sorbet into serving bowls and serve immediately.

Kiwi & Strawberry Sorbet

Prep time: 5 minutes | Cook time: 5 minutes | Serves 4

2 cups frozen sliced strawberries

4 kiwis, peeled and cut into 1-inch pieces

¼ cup agave nectar

¼ cup water

1. In a high-speed blender, add all the ingredients and pulse until smooth. 2. Transfer the mixture into an empty Ninja CREAMi pint container. 3. Cover the container with storage lid and freeze for 24 hours. 4. After 24 hours, remove the lid from container and arrange into the Outer Bowl of Ninja CREAMi. 5. Install the Creamerizer Paddle onto the lid of Outer Bowl. 6. Then rotate the lid clockwise to lock. 7. Press Power button to turn on the unit. 8. Then press Sorbet button. 9. When the program is completed, turn the Outer Bowl and release it from the machine. 10. Transfer the sorbet into serving bowls and serve immediately.

Cherry Sorbet

Prep time: 5 minutes | Cook time: 5 minutes | Serves 4

1½ cups cola

⅓ cup maraschino cherries

⅓ cup spiced rum

¼ cup water

1 tablespoon fresh lime juice

1. In a high-speed blender, add all the ingredients and pulse until smooth. 2. Transfer the mixture into an empty Ninja CREAMi pint container. 3. Cover the container with the storage lid and freeze for 24 hours. 4. After 24 hours, remove the lid from container and arrange into the outer bowl of Ninja CREAMi. 5. Install the "Creamerizer Paddle" onto the lid of outer bowl. 6. Then rotate the lid clockwise to lock. 7. Press "Power" button to turn on the unit. 8. Then press "SORBET" button. 9. When the program is completed, turn the outer bowl and release it from the machine. 10. Transfer the sorbet into serving bowls and serve immediately.

Strawberries & Champagne Sorbet

Prep time: 5 minutes | Cook time: 15 minutes | Serves 3
1 packet strawberry-flavored gelatin (such as Jell-O)
¾ cup boiling water
½ cup light corn syrup
3 fluid ounces champagne
1 egg whites, slightly beaten

1. Dissolve the gelatin in boiling water in a bowl. Beat in the corn syrup, champagne, and egg whites. 2. Put the mixture into the ninja CREAMi Pint container and freeze on a level surface in a cold freezer for a full 24 hours. 3. After 24 hours, remove the Pint from the freezer. Remove the lid. 4. Place the Ninja CREAMi Pint into the outer bowl. Place the outer bowl with the Pint in it into the ninja CREAMi machine and turn until the outer bowl locks into place. Push the SORBET button. During the SORBET function, the sorbet will mix together and become very creamy. This should take approximately 2 minutes. 5. Once the SORBET function has ended, turn the outer bowl and release it from the ninja CREAMi machine. 6. Your sorbet is ready to eat! Enjoy!

Mixed Berries Sorbet

Prep time: 5 minutes | Cook time: 5 minutes | Serves 4
1 cup blueberries
1 cup raspberries
1 cup strawberries, hulled and quartered

1. In an empty Ninja CREAMi pint container, place the berries and with a potato masher, mash until well combined. 2. Cover the container with storage lid and freeze for 24 hours. 3. After 24 hours, remove the lid from container and arrange into the outer bowl of Ninja CREAMi. 4. Install the Creamerizer Paddle onto the lid of Outer Bowl. 5. Then rotate the lid clockwise to lock. 6. Press Power button to turn on the unit. 7. Then press Sorbet button. 8. When the program is completed, turn the Outer Bowl and release it from the machine. 9. Transfer the sorbet into serving bowls and serve immediately.

Chapter 3 Milkshake Recipes

Chapter 3 Milkshake Recipes

Avocado Milkshake

Prep time: 5 minutes | Cook time: 5 minutes | Serves 2
1 cup coconut ice cream
1 small ripe avocado, peeled, pitted and chopped
1 teaspoon fresh lemon juice
2 tablespoons agave nectar
1 teaspoon vanilla extract
Pinch of salt
½ cup oat milk

1. In an empty Ninja CREAMi pint container, place ice cream, followed by remaining ingredients. 2. Arrange the container into the outer bowl of Ninja CREAMi. 3. Install the "Creamerizer Paddle" onto the lid of outer bowl. 4. Then rotate the lid clockwise to lock. 5. Press "Power" button to turn on the unit. 6. Then press "MILKSHAKE" button. 7. When the program is completed, turn the outer bowl and release it from the machine. 8. Transfer the shake into serving glasses and serve immediately.

Mocha Tahini Milkshake

Prep time: 5 minutes | Cook time: 3 minutes | Serves 2
1½ cups chocolate ice cream
½ cup unsweetened oat milk
¼ cup tahini
2 tablespoons coffee
1 tablespoon chocolate fudge

1. In an empty Ninja CREAMi pint container, place ice cream followed by milk, tahini, coffee and fudge. 2. Arrange the container into the Outer Bowl of Ninja CREAMi. 3. Install the Creamerizer Paddle onto the lid of Outer Bowl. 4. Then rotate the lid clockwise to lock. 5. Press Power button to turn on the unit. 6. Then press Milkshake button. 7. When the program is completed, turn the Outer Bowl and release it from the machine. 8. Transfer the shake into serving glasses and serve immediately.

Mocha Milkshake

Prep time: 5 minutes | Cook time: 3 minutes | Serves 2
1½ cups chocolate ice cream
½ cup cashew milk
½ cup ripe banana, peeled and cut into ½-inch pieces
1 tablespoon instant coffee powder

1. In an empty Ninja CREAMi pint container, place ice cream followed by milk, banana and coffee powder. 2. Arrange the container into the Outer Bowl of Ninja CREAMi. 3. Install the Creamerizer Paddle onto the lid of Outer Bowl. 4. Then rotate the lid clockwise to lock. 5. Press Power button to turn on the unit. 6. Then press Milkshake button. 7. When the program is completed, turn the Outer Bowl and release it from the machine. 8. Transfer the shake into serving glasses and serve immediately.

Chocolate Yogurt Milkshake

Prep time: 5 minutes | Cook time: 3 minutes | Serves 2
1 cup frozen chocolate yogurt
1 scoop chocolate whey protein powder
1 cup whole milk

1. In an empty Ninja CREAMi pint container, place yogurt followed by protein powder and milk. 2. Arrange the container into the Outer Bowl of Ninja CREAMi. 3. Install the Creamerizer Paddle onto the lid of Outer Bowl. 4. Then rotate the lid clockwise to lock. 5. Press Power button to turn on the unit. 6. Then press Milkshake button. 7. When the program is completed, turn the Outer Bowl and release it from the machine. 8. Transfer the shake into serving glasses and serve immediately.

Dairy-free Strawberry Milkshake

Prep time: 5 minutes | Cook time: 3 minutes | Serves 2
1½ cups Coconut-Vanilla Ice Cream
½ cup oat milk
3 fresh strawberries

1. Combine the ice cream, oat milk, and strawberries in a clean CREAMi Pint. 2. Place the pint in the outer bowl of your Ninja CREAMi, install the Creamerizer Paddle in the outer bowl lid, and lock the lid assembly onto the outer bowl. Place the bowl assembly on the motor base, and twist the handle to the right to raise the platform and lock it in place. Select the Milkshake function. 3. Once the machine has finished processing, remove the milkshake from the pint. Serve immediately.

Amaretto Cookies Milkshake

Prep time: 5 minutes | Cook time: 3 minutes | Serves 2
1 cup whole milk
½ cup amaretto-flavored coffee creamer
¼ cup amaretto liqueur
1 tablespoon agave nectar
¼ cup chocolate chip cookies, chopped

1. In an empty Ninja CREAMi pint container, place all ingredients except for cookies and stir to combine. 2. Cover the container with the storage lid and freeze for 24 hours. 3. After 24 hours, remove the lid from container and arrange into the outer bowl of Ninja CREAMi. 4. Install the "Creamerizer Paddle" onto the lid of outer bowl. 5. Then rotate the lid clockwise to lock. 6. Press "Power" button to turn on the unit. 7. Then press "MILKSHAKE" button. 8. When the program is completed, with a spoon, create a 1½-inch wide hole in the center that reaches the bottom of the pint container. 9. Add the chopped cookies into the hole and press "MIX-IN" button. 10. When the program is completed, turn the outer bowl and release it from the machine. 11. Transfer the shake into serving glasses and serve immediately.

Sugar Cookie Milkshake

Prep time: 8 minutes | Cook time: 5 minutes | Serves 1

½ cup vanilla ice cream

½ cup oat milk

3 small sugar cookies, crushed

2 tablespoons sprinkles

1. In an empty Ninja CREAMi pint container, place the ice cream. 2. With a spoon, create a 1½-inch wide hole in the center that reaches the bottom of the pint container. 3. Add the remaining ingredients into the hole. 4. Arrange the container into the outer bowl of Ninja CREAMi. 5. Install the "Creamerizer Paddle" onto the lid of outer bowl. 6. Then rotate the lid clockwise to lock. 7. Press "Power" button to turn on the unit. 8. Then press "MILKSHAKE" button. 9. When the program is completed, turn the outer bowl and release it from the machine. 10. Transfer the shake into a serving glass and serve immediately.

Healthy Strawberry Shake

Prep time: 5 minutes | Cook time: 10 minutes | Serves 1

1 cup milk

1 tablespoon honey

½ teaspoon vanilla extract

½ cup frozen strawberries

1. Add the milk, honey, vanilla extract, and strawberries into an empty CREAMi Pint. 2. Place Pint in outer bowl, install Creamerizer Paddle onto outer bowl lid and lock the lid assembly on the outer bowl. Place the bowl assembly on the motor base and crank the lever to elevate and secure the platform in place. 3. Select MILKSHAKE. 4. Remove the milkshake from the Pint after the processing is finished.

Lime Sherbet Milkshake

Prep time: 5 minutes | Cook time: 3 minutes | Serves 1

1½ cups rainbow sherbet

½ cup lime seltzer

1. In an empty Ninja CREAMi pint container, place sherbet and top with lime seltzer. 2. Arrange the container into the outer bowl of Ninja CREAMi. 3. Install the "Creamerizer Paddle" onto the lid of outer bowl. 4. Then rotate the lid clockwise to lock. 5. Press "Power" button to turn on the unit. 6. Then press "MILKSHAKE" button. 7. When the program is completed, turn the outer bowl and release it from the machine. 8. Transfer the shake into a serving glass and serve immediately.

Cashew Butter Milkshake

Prep time: 5 minutes | Cook time: 3 minutes | Serves 2

1½ cups vanilla ice cream

½ cup canned cashew milk

¼ cup cashew butter

1. In an empty Ninja CREAMi pint container, place the ice cream. 2. With a spoon, create a 1½-inch wide hole in the center that reaches the bottom of the pint container. 3. Add the remaining ingredients into the hole. 4. Arrange the container into the Outer Bowl of Ninja CREAMi. 5. Install the Creamerizer Paddle onto the lid of Outer Bowl. 6. Then rotate the lid clockwise to lock. 7. Press Power button to turn on the unit. 8. Then press Milkshake button. 9. When the program is completed, turn the Outer Bowl and release it from the machine. 10. Transfer the shake into serving glasses and serve immediately.

Cacao Mint Milkshake

Prep time: 5 minutes | Cook time: 3 minutes | Serves 2

1½ cups vanilla ice cream

½ cup canned full-fat coconut milk

1 teaspoon matcha powder

¼ cup cacao nibs

1 teaspoon peppermint extract

1. In an empty Ninja CREAMi pint container, place ice cream followed by coconut milk, matcha powder, cacao nibs and peppermint extract. 2. Arrange the container

into the Outer Bowl of Ninja CREAMi. 3. Install the Creamerizer Paddle onto the lid of Outer Bowl. 4. Then rotate the lid clockwise to lock. 5. Press Power button to turn on the unit. 6. Then press Milkshake button. 7. When the program is completed, turn the Outer Bowl and release it from the machine. 8. Transfer the shake into serving glasses and serve immediately.

Chocolate-hazelnut Milkshake

Prep time: 5 minutes | Cook time: 3 minutes | Serves 4
2 tablespoons granulated sugar
2 tablespoons unsweetened cocoa powder
½ cup whole milk
1 cup hazelnut-flavored coffee creamer

1. In a large bowl, whisk together the sugar, cocoa powder, milk, and coffee creamer until the sugar is fully dissolved. 2. Pour the base into a clean CREAMi Pint. Place the storage lid on the container and freeze for 24 hours. 3. Remove the pint from the freezer and take off the lid. Place the pint in the outer bowl of your Ninja CREAMi, install the Creamerizer Paddle in the outer bowl lid, and lock the lid assembly onto the outer bowl. Place the bowl assembly on the motor base, and twist the handle to the right to raise the platform and lock it in place. Select the Milkshake function. 4. Once the machine has finished processing, remove the milkshake from the pint. Serve immediately.

Cacao Matcha Milkshake

Prep time: 5 minutes | Cook time: 3 minutes | Serves 2
1½ cups vanilla ice cream
½ cup canned full-fat coconut milk
1 teaspoon matcha powder
¼ cup cacao nibs
¾ teaspoon peppermint extract
¼ teaspoon vanilla extract

1. In an empty Ninja CREAMi pint container, place ice cream, followed by coconut milk, matcha powder, cacao nibs and peppermint extract. 2. Arrange the container into the outer bowl of Ninja CREAMi. 3. Install the "Creamerizer Paddle" onto the lid of outer bowl. 4. Then rotate the lid clockwise to lock. 5. Press "Power" button to turn on the unit. 6. Then press "MILKSHAKE" button. 7. When the program is completed, turn the outer bowl and release it from the machine. 8. Transfer the

shake into serving glasses and serve immediately.

Lite Peanut Butter Ice Cream

Prep time: 5 minutes | Cook time: 3 minutes | Serves 4
1¾ cups fat-free (skim) milk
¼ cup stevia–cane sugar blend
1 teaspoon vanilla extract
3 tablespoons smooth peanut butter

1. In a medium bowl, whisk together the milk, stevia blend, vanilla extract, and peanut butter until the mixture is smooth and the stevia is fully dissolved. Let the mixture sit for about 5 minutes, until any foam subsides. If the stevia is still not dissolved, whisk again. 2. Pour the base into a clean CREAMi Pint. Place the storage lid on the container and freeze for 24 hours. 3. Remove the pint from the freezer and take off the lid. Place the pint in the outer bowl of your Ninja CREAMi, install the Creamerizer Paddle in the outer bowl lid, and lock the lid assembly onto the outer bowl. Place the bowl assembly on the motor base, and twist the handle to the right to raise the platform and lock it in place. Select the Lite Ice Cream function. 4. Once the machine has finished processing, remove the ice cream from the pint. Serve immediately.

Chocolate Hazelnut Milkshake

Prep time: 6 minutes | Cook time: 10 minutes | Serves 2
1 cup chocolate ice cream
½ cup whole milk
¼ cup hazelnut spread

1. Place the ice cream in an empty CREAMi Pint. 2. Create a 1½-inch-wide hole in the bottom of the Pint using a spoon. Fill the hole with the remaining ingredients. 3. Place Pint in outer bowl, install Creamerizer Paddle onto outer bowl lid and lock the lid assembly on the outer bowl. Place bowl assembly on motor base and twist the handle right to raise the platform and lock in place. 4. Select MILKSHAKE. 5. When the milkshake has finished processing, take it from the Pint and serve right away.

Chocolate Ginger Milkshake

Prep time: 5 minutes | Cook time: 3 minutes | Serves 2

1½ cups chocolate ice cream

½ cup oat milk

1 teaspoon ground ginger

¼ cup chocolate, grated

1. In an empty Ninja CREAMi pint container, place the ice cream. 2. With a spoon, create a 1½-inch wide hole in the center that reaches the bottom of the pint container. 3. Add the remaining ingredients into the hole. 4. Arrange the container into the outer bowl of Ninja CREAMi. 5. Install the "Creamerizer Paddle" onto the lid of outer bowl. 6. Then rotate the lid clockwise to lock. 7. Press "Power" button to turn on the unit. 8. Then press "MILKSHAKE" button. 9. When the program is completed, turn the outer bowl and release it from the machine. 10. Transfer the shake into serving glasses and serve immediately.

Chocolate Ice Cream Milkshake

Prep time: 5 minutes | Cook time: 3 minutes | Serves 1

1½ cups chocolate ice cream

½ cup whole milk

1. In an empty Ninja CREAMi pint container, place ice cream, followed by milk. 2. Arrange the container into the Outer Bowl of Ninja CREAMi. 3. Install the Creamerizer Paddle onto the lid of Outer Bowl. 4. Then rotate the lid clockwise to lock. 5. Press Power button to turn on the unit. 6. Then press Milkshake button. 7. When the program is completed, turn the Outer Bowl and release it from the machine. 8. Transfer the shake into a serving glass and serve immediately.

Frozen Mudslide

Prep time: 5 minutes | Cook time: 3 minutes | Serves 2

2 cups ice cubes

½ cup store-bought vanilla ice cream

6 tablespoons espresso vodka

6 tablespoons coffee-flavored liqueur

6 tablespoons Irish cream–flavored liqueur

1. Combine the ice, ice cream, vodka, and liqueurs in a blender. Blend on high until

smooth. 2. Pour the base into a clean CREAMi Pint. Place the storage lid on the container and freeze for 24 hours. 3. Remove the pint from the freezer and take off the lid. Place the pint in the outer bowl of your Ninja CREAMi, install the Creamerizer Paddle in the outer bowl lid, and lock the lid assembly onto the outer bowl. Place the bowl assembly on the motor base, and twist the handle to the right to raise the platform and lock it in place. Select the Milkshake function. 4. Once the machine has finished processing, remove the milkshake from the pint. Serve immediately.

Lemon Cookie Milkshake

Prep time: 8 minutes | Cook time: 3 minutes | Serves 2
1½ cups vanilla ice cream
3 lemon cream sandwich cookies
¼ cup milk

1. In an empty Ninja CREAMi pint container, place ice cream followed by cookies and milk. 2. Arrange the container into the Outer Bowl of Ninja CREAMi. 3. Install the Creamerizer Paddle onto the lid of Outer Bowl. 4. Then rotate the lid clockwise to lock. 5. Press Power button to turn on the unit. 6. Then press Milkshake button. 7. When the program is completed, turn the Outer Bowl and release it from the machine. 8. Transfer the shake into serving glasses and serve immediately.

Lemon Meringue Pie Milkshake

Prep time: 5 minutes | Cook time: 5 minutes | Serves 1
1 cup vanilla ice cream
4 tablespoons store-bought lemon curd, divided
4 tablespoons marshmallow topping, divided
½ cup Graham Crackers, broken, divided

1. Place the ice cream in an empty CREAMi Pint. 2. Use a spoon to create a 1½-inch wide hole that reaches the bottom of the Pint. Add the remaining ingredients to the hole. 3. Place Pint in outer bowl, install Creamerizer Paddle onto outer bowl lid and lock the lid assembly on the outer bowl. Place the bowl assembly on the motor base and crank the lever to elevate and secure the platform in place. 4. Select the MILKSHAKE option. 5. Remove the milkshake from the Pint after the processing is finished.

Chapter 4 Ice Cream Mix-ins

Chapter 4 Ice Cream Mix-ins

Fruity Cereal Ice Cream

Prep time: 5 minutes | Cook time: 30 minutes | Serves 2

¾ cup whole milk
1 cup fruity cereal, divided
1 tablespoon Philadelphia cream cheese, softened
¼ cup granulated sugar
1 teaspoon vanilla extract
½ cup heavy cream

1. In a large mixing bowl, combine ½ cup of the fruity cereal and the milk. Allow the mixture to settle for 15–30 minutes, stirring occasionally to infuse the milk with the fruity taste. 2. Microwave the Philadelphia cream cheese for 10 seconds in a second large microwave-safe dish. Combine the sugar and vanilla extract in a mixing bowl with a whisk or rubber spatula until the mixture resembles frosting, about 60 seconds. 3. After 15 to 30 minutes, sift the milk and cereal into the bowl with the sugar mixture using a fine-mesh filter. To release extra milk, press on the cereal with a spoon, then discard it. Mix in the heavy cream until everything is thoroughly mixed. 4. Pour the mixture into an empty ninja CREAMi Pint container. Add the strawberries to the Pint, making sure not to go over the max fill line, and freeze for 24 hours. 5. After 24 hours, remove the Pint from the freezer. Remove the lid. 6. Place the Ninja CREAMi Pint into the outer bowl. Place the outer bowl with the Pint in it into the ninja CREAMi machine and turn until the outer bowl locks into place. Push the ICE CREAM button. During the ICE CREAM function, the ice cream will mix together and become very creamy. 7. Use a spoon to create a 1½-inch wide hole that reaches the bottom of the Pint. Add the remaining ½ cup of fruity cereal to the hole and process again using the mix-in. When processing is complete, remove the ice cream from the Pint.

Rocky Road Ice Cream

Prep time: 5 minutes | Cook time: 3 minutes | Serves 4
1 cup whole milk
½ cup frozen cauliflower florets, thawed
½ cup dark brown sugar
3 tablespoons dark cocoa powder
1 teaspoon chocolate extract
⅓ cup heavy cream
2 tablespoons almonds, sliced
2 tablespoons mini marshmallows
2 tablespoons mini chocolate chips

1. 1n a high-speed blender, add milk, cauliflower, brown sugar, cocoa powder, and chocolate extract and pulse until smooth. 2. Transfer the mixture into an empty Ninja CREAMi pint container. 3. Add the heavy cream and stir until well combined. 4. Cover the container with storage lid and freeze for 24 hours. 5. After 24 hours, remove the lid from container and arrange into the Outer Bowl of Ninja CREAMi. 6. Install the Creamerizer Paddle onto the lid of Outer Bowl. 7. Then rotate the lid clockwise to lock. 8. Press Power button to turn on the unit. 9. Then press Ice Cream button. 10. When the program is completed, with a spoon, create a 1½-inch wide hole in the center that reaches the bottom of the pint container. 11. Add the almonds, marshmallows and chocolate chips into the hole and press Mix-In button. 12. When the program is completed, turn the Outer Bowl and release it from the machine. 13. Transfer the ice cream into serving bowls and serve immediately.

Cookies & Cream Ice Cream

Prep time: 5 minutes | Cook time: 5 minutes | Serves 2
½ tablespoon cream cheese, softened
¼ cup granulated sugar
½ teaspoon vanilla extract
½ cup heavy cream
½ cup whole milk
1½ chocolate sandwich cookies, broken, for mix-in

1. Microwave the cream cheese for 10 seconds in a large microwave-safe bowl. Combine the sugar and vanilla extract in a mixing bowl and whisk or scrape together until the mixture resembles frosting, about 60 seconds. 2. Slowly whisk in the heavy cream and milk until smooth and the sugar has dissolved. 3. Pour the

base into an empty CREAMi Pint. Place storage lid on the Pint and freeze for 24 hours. 4. Remove the Pint from the freezer and remove the lid from the Pint. Place the Pint in the outer bowl, install Creamerizer Paddle onto the outer bowl lid, and lock the lid assembly on the outer bowl. Select ICE CREAM. 5. With a spoon, create a 1½-inch wide hole that reaches the bottom of the Pint. During this process, it's okay for your treat to go above the max fill line. Add the broken chocolate sandwich cookies to the hole and process again using the MIX-IN program. 6. When processing is complete, remove the ice cream from the Pint and serve immediately.

Sneaky Mint Chip Ice Cream

Prep time: 5 minutes | Cook time: 3 minutes | Serves 4

3 large egg yolks
1 tablespoon corn syrup
¼ cup granulated sugar
⅓ cup whole milk
¾ cup heavy (whipping) cream
1 cup packed fresh spinach
½ cup frozen peas, thawed
1 teaspoon mint extract
¼ cup semisweet chocolate chips

1. Fill a large bowl with ice water and set it aside. 2. In a small saucepan, whisk together the egg yolks, corn syrup, and sugar until the mixture is fully combined and the sugar is dissolved. Do not do this over heat. 3. Whisk in the milk and heavy cream. 4. Place the pan over medium heat. Cook, stirring constantly with a rubber spatula, until the temperature reaches 165°F to 175°F on an instant-read thermometer. 5. Remove the pan from the heat and pour the base into a clean CREAMi Pint. Carefully place the container in the prepared ice water bath, making sure the water doesn't spill into the base. 6. Once the mixture has completely cooled, pour the base into a blender and add the spinach, peas, and mint extract. Blend on high for 30 seconds. Strain the base through a fine-mesh strainer back into the CREAMi Pint. Place the storage lid on the container and freeze for 24 hours. 7. Remove the pint from the freezer and take off the lid. Place the pint in the outer bowl of your Ninja CREAMi, install the Creamerizer Paddle in the outer bowl lid, and lock the lid assembly onto the outer bowl. Place the bowl assembly on the motor base, and twist the handle to the right to raise the platform and lock it in place. Select the Ice Cream function. 8. Once the machine has finished processing, remove the lid from the pint container. With a spoon, create a 1½-inch-wide hole that reaches the bottom of the pint. During this process, it is okay if your treat reaches above the Max Fill line. Add the chocolate chips to the hole in the pint,

replace the lid, and select the Mix-In function. 9. Once the machine has finished processing, remove the ice cream from the pint. Serve immediately.

Sweet Potato Pie Ice Cream

Prep time: 5 minutes | Cook time: 3 minutes | Serves 4
1 cup canned pureed sweet potato
1 tablespoon corn syrup
¼ cup plus 1 tablespoon light brown sugar
1 teaspoon vanilla extract
1 teaspoon cinnamon
¾ cup heavy (whipping) cream
¼ cup mini marshmallows

1. Combine the sweet potato puree, corn syrup, brown sugar, vanilla, and cinnamon in a blender. Blend on high until smooth. 2. Pour the base into a clean CREAMi Pint. Whisk in the heavy cream until combined. Place the storage lid on the container and freeze for 24 hours. 3. Remove the pint from the freezer and take off the lid. Place the pint in the outer bowl of your Ninja CREAMi, install the Creamerizer Paddle in the outer bowl lid, and lock the lid assembly onto the outer bowl. Place the bowl assembly on the motor base, and twist the handle to the right to raise the platform and lock it in place. Select the Ice Cream function. 4. Once the machine has finished processing, remove the lid from the pint container. With a spoon, create a 1½-inch-wide hole that reaches the bottom of the pint. During this process, it is okay if your treat reaches above the Max Fill line. Add the marshmallows to the hole in the pint, replace the lid, and select the Mix-In function. 5. Once the machine has finished processing, remove the ice cream from the pint. Serve immediately with desired toppings.

Snack Mix Ice Cream

Prep time: 5 minutes | Cook time: 10 seconds | Serves 4
1 tablespoon cream cheese, softened
⅓ cup granulated sugar
½ teaspoon vanilla extract
1 cup whole milk
¾ cup heavy cream
2 tablespoons sugar cone pieces
1 tablespoon mini pretzels
1 tablespoon potato chips, crushed

1. In a large microwave-safe bowl, add the cream cheese and microwave on High for about ten seconds. 2. Remove from the microwave and stir until smooth. 3. Add the sugar and vanilla extract and with a wire whisk, beat until the mixture looks like frosting. 4. Slowly add the milk and heavy cream and beat until well combined. 5. Transfer the mixture into an empty Ninja CREAMi pint container. 6. Cover the container with storage lid and freeze for 24 hours. 7. After 24 hours, remove the lid from container and arrange into the Outer Bowl of Ninja CREAMi. 8. Install the Creamerizer Paddle onto the lid of Outer Bowl. 9. Then rotate the lid clockwise to lock. 10. Press Power button to turn on the unit. 11. Then press Ice Cream button. 12. When the program is completed, with a spoon, create a 1½-inch wide hole in the center that reaches the bottom of the pint container. 13. Add the cone pieces, pretzels and potato chips into the hole and press Mix-In button. 14. When the program is completed, turn the Outer Bowl and release it from the machine. 15. Transfer the ice cream into serving bowls and serve immediately.

Pistachio Ice Cream

Prep time: 5 minutes | Cook time: 3 minutes | Serves 4
1 tablespoon cream cheese, softened
⅓ cup granulated sugar
1 teaspoon almond extract
1 cup whole milk
¾ cup heavy cream
¼ cup pistachios, shells removed and chopped

1. In a large microwave-safe bowl, add the cream cheese and microwave on High for about ten seconds. 2. Remove from the microwave and stir until smooth. 3. Add the sugar and almond extract and with a wire whisk, beat until the mixture looks

like frosting. 4. Slowly add the milk and heavy cream and beat until well combined. 5. Transfer the mixture into an empty Ninja CREAMi pint container. 6. Cover the container with storage lid and freeze for 24 hours. 7. After 24 hours, remove the lid from container and arrange into the Outer Bowl of Ninja CREAMi. 8. Install the Creamerizer Paddle onto the lid of Outer Bowl. 9. Then rotate the lid clockwise to lock. 10. Press Power button to turn on the unit. 11. Then press Ice Cream button. 12. When the program is completed, with a spoon, create a 1½-inch wide hole in the center that reaches the bottom of the pint container. 13. Add the pistachios into the hole and press Mix-In button. 14. When the program is completed, turn the Outer Bowl and release it from the machine. 15. Transfer the ice cream into serving bowls and serve immediately.

Jelly & Peanut Butter Ice Cream

Prep time: 5 minutes | Cook time: 5 minutes | Serves 4
3 tablespoons granulated sugar
4 large egg yolks
1 cup whole milk
⅓ cup heavy cream
¼ cup smooth peanut butter
3 tablespoons grape jelly
¼ cup honey roasted peanuts, chopped

1. In a small saucepan, add the sugar and egg yolks and beat until sugar is dissolved. 2. Add the milk, heavy cream, peanut butter, and grape jelly to the saucepan and stir to combine. 3. Place saucepan over medium heat and cook until temperature reaches cook until temperature reaches to 165 -175° F, stirring continuously with a rubber spatula. 4. Remove from the heat and through a fine-mesh strainer, strain the mixture into an empty Ninja CREAMi pint container. 5. Place the container into ice bath to cool. 6. After cooling, cover the container with storage lid and freeze for 24 hours. 7. After 24 hours, remove the lid from container and arrange into the Outer Bowl of Ninja CREAMi. 8. Install the Creamerizer Paddle onto the lid of Outer Bowl. 9. Then rotate the lid clockwise to lock. 10. Press Power button to turn on the unit. 11. Then press ICE CREAM button. 12. When the program is completed, with a spoon, create a 1½-inch wide hole in the center that reaches the bottom of the pint container. 13. Add the peanuts into the hole and press Mix-In button. 14. When the program is completed, turn the Outer Bowl and release it from the machine. 15. Transfer the ice cream into serving bowls and serve immediately.

Coffee And Cookies Ice Cream

Prep time: 5 minutes | Cook time: 3 minutes | Serves 4
1 tablespoon cream cheese, at room temperature
⅓ cup granulated sugar
1 teaspoon vanilla extract
1 tablespoon instant espresso
¾ cup heavy (whipping) cream
1 cup whole milk
¼ cup crushed chocolate sandwich cookies

1. In a large bowl, whisk together the cream cheese, sugar, and vanilla for about 1 minute, until the mixture looks like frosting. 2. Slowly whisk in the instant espresso, heavy cream, and milk until fully combined. 3. Pour the base into a clean CREAMi Pint. Place the lid on the container and freeze for 24 hours. 4. Remove the pint from the freezer and take off the lid. Place the pint in the outer bowl of your Ninja CREAMi, install the Creamerizer Paddle in the outer bowl lid, and lock the lid assembly onto the outer bowl. Place the bowl assembly on the motor base, and twist the handle to the right to raise the platform and lock it in place. Select the Ice Cream function. 5. Once the machine has finished processing, remove the lid from the pint container. With a spoon, create a 1½-inch-wide hole that reaches the bottom of the pint. Add the crushed cookies to the hole, replace the lid, and select the Mix-In function. 6. Once the machine has finished processing, remove the ice cream from the pint. Serve immediately.

Coconut Mint Chip Ice Cream

Prep time: 5 minutes | Cook time: 3 minutes | Serves 4
1 can full-fat unsweetened coconut milk
½ cup organic sugar
½ teaspoon mint extract
¼ cup mini vegan chocolate chips

1. In a medium bowl, whisk together the coconut milk, sugar, and mint extract until everything is well combined and the sugar is dissolved. 2. Pour the base into a clean CREAMi Pint. Place the storage lid on the container and freeze for 24 hours. 3. Remove the pint from the freezer and take off the lid. Place the pint in the outer bowl of your Ninja CREAMi, install the Creamerizer Paddle in the outer bowl lid, and lock the lid assembly onto the outer bowl. Place the bowl assembly on the motor base, and twist the handle to the right to raise the platform and lock it in

place. Select the Ice Cream function. 4. Once the machine has finished processing, remove the lid from the pint container. With a spoon, create a 1½-inch-wide hole that reaches the bottom of the pint. During this process, it is okay if your treat reaches above the Max Fill line. Add the mini chocolate chips to the hole in the pint, replace the lid, and select the Mix-In function. 5. Once the machine has finished processing, remove the ice cream from the pint. Serve immediately with desired toppings.

Cookies And Coconut Ice Cream

Prep time: 5 minutes | Cook time: 3 minutes | Serves 4
1 can full-fat unsweetened coconut milk
½ cup organic sugar
1 teaspoon vanilla extract
4 chocolate sandwich cookies, crushed

1. In a medium bowl, whisk together the coconut milk, sugar, and vanilla until well combined and the sugar is dissolved. 2. Pour the base into a clean CREAMi Pint. Place the storage lid on the container and freeze for 24 hours. 3. Remove the pint from the freezer and take off the lid. Place the pint in the outer bowl of your Ninja CREAMi, install the Creamerizer Paddle in the outer bowl lid, and lock the lid assembly onto the outer bowl. Place the bowl assembly on the motor base, and twist the handle to the right to raise the platform and lock it in place. Select the Ice Cream function. 4. Once the machine has finished processing, remove the lid from the pint container. With a spoon, create a 1½-inch-wide hole that reaches the bottom of the pint. During this process, it is okay if your treat reaches above the Max Fill line. Add the crushed cookies to the hole in the pint, replace the lid, and select the Mix-In function. 5. Once the machine has finished processing, remove the ice cream from the pint. Serve immediately with desired toppings.

Rum Raisin Ice Cream

Prep time: 5 minutes | Cook time: 23 minutes | Serves 4
3 large egg yolks
¼ cup dark brown sugar (or coconut sugar)
1 tablespoon light corn syrup
½ cup heavy cream
1 cup whole milk
1 teaspoon rum extract
⅓ cup raisins
¼ cup dark or spiced rum

1. In a small saucepan, combine the egg yolks, sugar, and corn syrup. Whisk until everything is well mixed and the sugar has dissolved. Whisk together the heavy cream and milk until smooth. 2. Stir the mixture frequently with a whisk or a rubber spatula in a saucepan over medium-low heat. Using an instant-read thermometer, cook until the temperature hits 165°F–175°F. 3. Remove the base from heat, stir in the rum extract, then pour through a fine-mesh strainer into an empty CREAMi Pint. Place into an ice bath. Once cooled, place the storage lid on the Pint and freeze for 24 hours. 4. While the base is cooling, prepare the mix-in. Add the raisins and rum to a small bowl and microwave for 1 minute. Let cool, then drain the remaining rum. Cover and set aside. 5. Remove the Pint from the freezer and remove its lid. Place the Pint in the outer bowl, install the Creamerizer Paddle onto the outer bowl lid, and lock the lid assembly on the outer bowl. Select ICE CREAM. 6. With a spoon, create a 1½-inch wide hole that reaches the bottom of the Pint. Add the mixed raisins to the hole and process again using the MIX-IN program. 7. When processing is complete, remove the ice cream from the Pint.

Mint Chocolate Chip Ice Cream

Prep time: 5 minutes | Cook time: 5 minutes | Serves 4
1 tablespoon cream cheese, softened
⅓ cup granulated sugar
1 teaspoon vanilla extract
¾ cup heavy cream
1 cup whole milk
1 teaspoon mint extract
Green food coloring (optional)
¼ cup mini chocolate chips, for mix-in

1. Microwave the cream cheese for 10 seconds in a large microwave-safe bowl. Combine with the sugar and mint extract in a mixing bowl using a whisk or rubber spatula for about 60 seconds or until the mixture resembles frosting. 2. Slowly whisk in the heavy cream, milk, and optional food coloring until thoroughly mixed and the sugar has dissolved. 3. Pour the base into an empty CREAMi Pint. Place the storage lid on the Pint and freeze for 24 hours. 4. Remove the Pint from the freezer and remove its lid. Place the Pint in the outer bowl, install the Creamerizer Paddle onto the outer bowl lid, and lock the lid assembly on the outer bowl. Place the bowl assembly on the motor base, twist the handle to raise the platform, and lock it in place. 5. Select ICE CREAM. 6.With a spoon, create a 1½-inch wide hole that reaches the bottom of the Pint. During this process, it's okay for your treat to press above the max fill line. Add the chocolate chips to the hole and process again using the MIX-IN program.

Lavender Cookies & Cream Ice Cream

Prep time: 8 minutes | Cook time: 20 minutes | Serves 2
½ cup heavy cream
½ tablespoon dried culinary lavender
¼ teaspoon kosher salt
½ cup whole milk
¼ cup sweetened condensed milk
2 drops purple food coloring
¼ cup crushed chocolate wafer cookies

1. Whisk together the heavy cream, lavender, and salt in a medium saucepan. 2. Steep the mixture for 10 minutes over low heat, stirring every 2 minutes to prevent bubbling. 3. Using a fine-mesh strainer, drain the lavender from the heavy cream into a large mixing basin. Discard the lavender. 4. Combine the milk, sweetened condensed milk, and purple food coloring in a large mixing bowl. Whisk until the mixture is completely smooth. 5. Pour the base into an empty CREAMi Pint. Place the Pint into an ice bath. Once cooled, place the storage lid on the Pint and freeze for 24 hours. 6. Remove the Pint from the freezer and remove its lid. Place Pint in outer bowl, install Creamerizer Paddle in outer bowl lid, and lock the lid assembly onto the outer bowl. Select ICE CREAM. 7. When the process is done, create a 1½-inch wide hole that reaches the bottom of the Pint with a spoon. It's okay if your treat exceeds the max fill line. Add crushed wafer cookies to the hole and process again using the MIX-IN program. 8. When processing is complete, remove ice cream from Pint and serve immediately, topped with extra crumbled wafers if desired.

Mint Cookies Ice Cream

Prep time: 5 minutes | Cook time: 3 minutes | Serves 4
¾ cup coconut cream
¼ cup monk fruit sweetener with Erythritol
2 tablespoons agave nectar
½ teaspoon mint extract
5-6 drops green food coloring
1 cup oat milk
3 chocolate sandwich cookies, quartered

1. 1n a large bowl, add the coconut cream and beat until smooth. 2. Add the sweetener, agave nectar, mint extract and food coloring and beat until sweetener is dissolved. 3. Add the oat milk and beat until well combined. 4. Transfer the mixture into an empty Ninja CREAMi pint container. 5. Cover the container with storage lid and freeze for 24 hours. 6. After 24 hours, remove the lid from container and arrange into the Outer Bowl of Ninja CREAMi. 7. Install the Creamerizer Paddle onto the lid of Outer Bowl. 8. Then rotate the lid clockwise to lock. 9. Press Power button to turn on the unit. 10. Then press Lite Ice Cream button. 11. When the program is completed, with a spoon, create a 1½-inch wide hole in the center that reaches the bottom of the pint container. 12. Add the cookie pieces into the hole and press Mix-In button. 13. When the program is completed, turn the Outer Bowl and release it from the machine. 14. Transfer the ice cream into serving bowls and serve immediately.

Lite Chocolate Cookie Ice Cream

Prep time: 5 minutes | Cook time: 5 minutes | Serves 2
1 tablespoon cream cheese, at room temperature
2 tablespoons unsweetened cocoa powder
½ teaspoon stevia sweetener
3 tablespoons raw agave nectar
1 teaspoon vanilla extract
¾ cup heavy cream
1 cup whole milk
¼ cup crushed reduced-fat sugar cookies

1. Place the cream cheese in a large microwave-safe bowl and heat on high for 10 seconds. 2. Mix in the cocoa powder, stevia, agave, and vanilla. Microwave for 60 seconds more, or until the mixture resembles frosting. 3. Slowly whisk in the heavy

cream and milk until the sugar has dissolved and the mixture is thoroughly mixed. 4. Pour the base into a clean CREAMi Pint. Place the storage lid on the container and freeze for 24 hours. 5. Remove the Pint from the freezer and take off the lid. Place the Pint in the outer bowl of your Ninja CREAMi, install the Creamerizer Paddle in the outer bowl lid, and lock the lid assembly onto the outer bowl. Place the bowl assembly on the motor base, and twist the handle to the right to raise the platform and lock it in place. Select the LITE ICE CREAM function. 6. Once the machine has finished processing, remove the lid. With a spoon, create a 1½-inch-wide hole that reaches the bottom of the Pint. During this process, it's okay if your treat goes above the max fill line. Add the crushed cookies to the hole in the Pint. Replace the Pint lid and select the MIX-IN function. 7. Once the machine has finished processing, remove the ice cream from the Pint.

Birthday Cake Ice Cream

Prep time: 5 minutes | Cook time: 3 minutes | Serves 4
5 large egg yolks
¼ cup corn syrup
2½ tablespoons granulated sugar
⅓ cup whole milk
1 cup heavy (whipping) cream
1½ tablespoons vanilla extract
3 tablespoons vanilla cake mix
2 tablespoons rainbow-colored sprinkles

1. Fill a large bowl with ice water and set it aside. 2. In a small saucepan, whisk together the egg yolks, corn syrup, and sugar until the mixture is fully combined and the sugar is dissolved. Do not do this over heat. 3. Whisk in the milk, heavy cream, and vanilla. 4. Place the pan over medium heat. Cook, stirring constantly with a rubber spatula, until the temperature reaches 165°F to 175°F on an instant-read thermometer. 5. Remove the pan from the heat and pour the base through a fine-mesh strainer into a clean CREAMi Pint. Carefully place the container in the prepared ice water bath, making sure the water doesn't spill into the base. 6. Once the base has cooled, whisk in the vanilla cake mix until it is fully incorporated. Place the storage lid on the pint container and freeze for 24 hours. 7. Remove the pint from the freezer and take off the lid. Place the pint in the outer bowl of your Ninja CREAMi, install the Creamerizer Paddle in the outer bowl lid, and lock the lid assembly onto the outer bowl. Place the bowl assembly on the motor base, and twist the handle to the right to raise the platform and lock it in place. Select the Ice Cream function. 8. Once the machine has finished processing, remove the lid from the pint container. With a spoon, create a 1½-inch-wide hole

that reaches the bottom of the pint. During this process, it is okay if your treat reaches above the Max Fill line. Add the rainbow sprinkles to the hole in the pint, replace the lid, and select the Mix-In function. 9. Once the machine has finished processing, remove the ice cream from the pint. Serve immediately.

Grasshopper Ice Cream

Prep time: 5 minutes | Cook time: 3 minutes | Serves 4
½ cup frozen spinach, thawed and squeezed dry
1 cup whole milk
½ cup granulated sugar
1 teaspoon mint extract
3-5 drops green food coloring
⅓ cup heavy cream
¼ cup chocolate chunks, chopped
¼ cup brownie, cut into 1-inch pieces

1. In a high-speed blender, add the spinach, milk, sugar, mint extract and food coloring and pulse until mixture smooth. 2. Transfer the mixture into an empty Ninja CREAMi pint container. 3. Add the heavy cream and stir until well combined. 4. Cover the container with storage lid and freeze for 24 hours. 5. After 24 hours, remove the lid from container and arrange into the Outer Bowl of Ninja CREAMi. 6. Install the Creamerizer Paddle onto the lid of Outer Bowl. 7. Then rotate the lid clockwise to lock. 8. Press Power button to turn on the unit. 9. Then press Ice Cream button. 10. When the program is completed, with a spoon, create a 1½-inch wide hole in the center that reaches the bottom of the pint container. 11. Add the chocolate chunks and brownie pieces into the hole and press Mix-In button. 12. When the program is completed, turn the Outer Bowl and release it from the machine. 13. Transfer the ice cream into serving bowls and serve immediately.

Triple-chocolate Ice Cream

Prep time: 5 minutes | Cook time: 3 minutes | Serves 4

4 large egg yolks
⅓ cup granulated sugar
1 tablespoon unsweetened cocoa powder
1 tablespoon hot fudge sauce
¾ cup heavy (whipping) cream
½ cup whole milk
1 teaspoon vanilla extract
¼ cup white chocolate chips

1. Fill a large bowl with ice water and set it aside. 2. In a small saucepan, whisk together the egg yolks, sugar, and cocoa powder until the mixture is fully combined and the sugar is dissolved. Do not do this over heat. 3. Whisk in the hot fudge, heavy cream, milk, and vanilla. 4. Place the pan over medium heat. Cook, stirring constantly with a rubber spatula, until the temperature reaches 165°F to 175°F on an instant-read thermometer. 5. Remove the pan from the heat and pour the base through a fine-mesh strainer into a clean CREAMi Pint. Carefully place the container in the prepared ice water bath, making sure the water doesn't spill into the base. 6. Once the base has cooled, place the storage lid on the pint and freeze for 24 hours. 7. Remove the pint from the freezer and take off the lid. Place the pint in the outer bowl of your Ninja CREAMi, install the Creamerizer Paddle in the outer bowl lid, and lock the lid assembly onto the outer bowl. Place the bowl assembly on the motor base, and twist the handle to the right to raise the platform and lock it in place. Select the Ice Cream function. 8. Once the machine has finished processing, remove the lid from the pint container. With a spoon, create a 1½-inch-wide hole that reaches the bottom of the pint. During this process, it is okay if your treat reaches above the Max Fill line. Add the white chocolate chips to the hole in the pint, replace the lid, and select the Mix-In function. 9. Once the machine has finished processing, remove the ice cream from the pint. Serve immediately with desired toppings.

Lavender Cookie Ice Cream

Prep time: 5 minutes | Cook time: 10 minutes | Serves 4

¾ cup heavy cream
1 tablespoon dried culinary lavender
⅛ teaspoon salt
¾ cup whole milk
½ cup sweetened condensed milk
4 drops purple food coloring
⅓ cup chocolate wafer cookies, crushed

1. In a medium saucepan, add heavy cream, lavender and salt and mix well. 2. Place the saucepan over low heat and steep, covered for about ten minutes, stirring after every two minutes. 3. Remove from the heat and through a fine-mesh strainer, strain the cream mixture into a large bowl. 4. Discard the lavender leaves. 5. In the bowl of cream mixture, add the milk, condensed milk and purple food coloring and beat until smooth. 6. Transfer the mixture into an empty Ninja CREAMi pint container. 7. Cover the container with storage lid and freeze for 24 hours. 8. After 24 hours, remove the lid from container and arrange into the Outer Bowl of Ninja CREAMi. 9. Install the Creamerizer Paddle onto the lid of Outer Bowl. 10. Then rotate the lid clockwise to lock. 11. Press Power button to turn on the unit. 12. Then press Ice Cream button. 13. When the program is completed, with a spoon, create a 1½-inch wide hole in the center that reaches the bottom of the pint container. 14. Add the crushed cookies the hole and press Mix-In button. 15. When the program is completed, turn the Outer Bowl and release it from the machine. 16. Transfer the ice cream into serving bowls and serve immediately.

Chapter 5 Gelato Recipes

Chapter 5 Gelato Recipes

Tiramisu Gelato

Prep time: 15 minutes | Cook time: 6 minutes | Serves 4
4 large egg yolks
⅓ cup granulated sugar
1 cup whole milk
⅓ cup heavy (whipping) cream
¼ cup cream cheese
1 tablespoon instant coffee
1 teaspoon rum extract
¼ cup ladyfinger pieces

1. Fill a large bowl with ice water and set it aside. 2. In a small saucepan, whisk together the egg yolks and sugar until the mixture is fully combined and the sugar is dissolved. Do not do this over heat. 3. Whisk in the milk, heavy cream, cream cheese, instant coffee, and rum extract. 4. Place the pan over medium heat. Cook, stirring constantly with a rubber spatula, until the temperature reaches 165°F to 175°F on an instant-read thermometer. 5. Remove the pan from the heat and pour the base through a fine-mesh strainer into a clean CREAMi Pint. Carefully place the container in the prepared ice water bath, making sure the water doesn't spill into the base. 6. Once the base has cooled, place the storage lid on the pint and freeze for 24 hours. 7. Remove the pint from the freezer and take off the lid. Place the pint in the outer bowl of your Ninja CREAMi, install the Creamerizer Paddle in the outer bowl lid, and lock the lid assembly onto the outer bowl. Place the bowl assembly on the motor base, and twist the handle to the right to raise the platform and lock it in place. Select the Gelato function. 8. Once the machine has finished processing, remove the lid from the pint container. With a spoon, create a 1½-inch-wide hole that reaches the bottom of the pint. During this process, it is okay if your treat reaches above the Max Fill line. Add the ladyfinger pieces to the hole in the pint, replace the lid, and select the Mix-In function. 9. Once the machine has finished processing, remove the gelato from the pint. Serve immediately.

Pumpkin Gelato

Prep time: 5 minutes | Cook time: 3 minutes | Serves 4

3 large egg yolks
⅓ cup granulated sugar
1 tablespoon light corn syrup
1 cup whole milk
½ cup heavy cream
½ cup canned pumpkin puree
1½ teaspoons pumpkin pie spice
1 teaspoon vanilla extract

1. In a small saucepan, add the egg yolks, sugar and corn syrup and beat until well combined. 2. Add the milk, heavy cream, pumpkin puree and pumpkin pie spice and beat until well combined. 3. Place the saucepan over medium heat and cook for about 2-3 minutes, stirring continuously. 4. Remove from the heat and stir in the vanilla extract. 5. Through a fine-mesh strainer, strain the mixture into an empty Ninja CREAMi pint container. 6. Place the container into an ice bath to cool. 7. After cooling, cover the container with the storage lid and freeze for 24 hours. 8. After 24 hours, remove the lid from container and arrange into the outer bowl of Ninja CREAMi. 9. Install the "Creamerizer Paddle" onto the lid of outer bowl. 10. Then rotate the lid clockwise to lock. 11. Press "Power" button to turn on the unit. 12. Then press "GELATO" button. 13. When the program is completed, turn the outer bowl and release it from the machine. 14. Transfer the gelato into serving bowls and serve immediately.

Pistachio Gelato

Prep time: 5 minutes | Cook time: 3 minutes | Serves 4

4 large egg yolks
¼ cup plus 1 tablespoon granulated sugar
1 tablespoon light corn syrup
⅓ cup whole milk
1 cup heavy (whipping) cream
1 teaspoon almond extract
5 drops green food coloring
¼ cup roasted pistachios

1. Fill a large bowl with ice water and set it aside. 2. In a small saucepan, whisk together the egg yolks, sugar, and corn syrup until the mixture is fully combined

and the sugar is dissolved. Do not do this over heat. 3. Whisk in the milk, heavy cream, almond extract, and food coloring. 4. Place the pan over medium heat. Cook, stirring constantly with a rubber spatula, until the temperature reaches 165°F to 175°F on an instant-read thermometer. 5. Remove the pan from the heat and pour the base through a fine-mesh strainer into a clean CREAMi Pint. Carefully place the container in the prepared ice water bath, making sure the water doesn't spill into the base. 6. Once the base has cooled, place the storage lid on the pint and freeze for 24 hours. 7. Remove the pint from the freezer and take off the lid. Place the pint in the outer bowl of your Ninja CREAMi, install the Creamerizer Paddle in the outer bowl lid, and lock the lid assembly onto the outer bowl. Place the bowl assembly on the motor base, and twist the handle to the right to raise the platform and lock it in place. Select the Gelato function. 8. Once the machine has finished processing, remove the lid from the pint container. With a spoon, create a 1½-inch-wide hole that reaches the bottom of the pint. During this process, it is okay if your treat reaches above the Max Fill line. Add the pistachios to the hole in the pint, replace the lid, and select the Mix-In function. 9. Once the machine has finished processing, remove the gelato from the pint. Serve immediately.

Blueberry & Crackers Gelato

Prep time: 10 minutes | Cook time: 3 minutes | Serves 4
4 large egg yolks
3 tablespoons granulated sugar
3 tablespoons wild blueberry preserves
1 teaspoon vanilla extract
1 cup whole milk
⅓ cup heavy cream
¼ cup cream cheese, softened
3-6 drops purple food coloring
2 large graham crackers, broken in 1-inch pieces

1. In a small saucepan, add the egg yolks, sugar, blueberry preserves and vanilla extract and beat until well combined. 2. Add the milk, heavy cream, cream cheese and food coloring and beat until well combined. 3. Place the saucepan over medium heat and cook for about 2-3 minutes, stirring continuously. 4. Remove from the heat and through a fine-mesh strainer, strain the mixture into an empty Ninja CREAMi pint container. 5. Place the container into an ice bath to cool. 6. After cooling, cover the container with the storage lid and freeze for 24 hours. 7. After 24 hours, remove the lid from container and arrange into the outer bowl of Ninja CREAMi. 8. Install the "Creamerizer Paddle" onto the lid of outer bowl. 9. Then rotate the lid clockwise to lock. 10. Press "Power" button to turn on the unit.

11. Then press "GELATO" button. 12. When the program is completed, with a spoon, create a 1½-inch wide hole in the center that reaches the bottom of the pint container. 13. Add the graham crackers into the hole and press "MIX-IN" button. 14. When the program is completed, turn the outer bowl and release it from the machine. 15. Transfer the gelato into serving bowls and serve immediately.

Maple Gelato

Prep time: 5 minutes | Cook time: 3 minutes | Serves 4
4 large egg yolks
½ cup plus 1 tablespoon light brown sugar
1 tablespoon maple syrup
1 teaspoon maple extract
1 cup whole milk
⅓ cup heavy cream

1. In a small saucepan, add the egg yolks, brown sugar, maple syrup and maple extract and beat until well combined. 2. Add the milk and heavy cream and beat until well combined. 3. Place the saucepan over medium heat and cook for about 2-3 minutes, stirring continuously. 4. Remove from the heat and through a fine-mesh strainer, strain the mixture into an empty Ninja CREAMi pint container. 5. Place the container into an ice bath to cool. 6. After cooling, cover the container with the storage lid and freeze for 24 hours. 7. After 24 hours, remove the lid from container and arrange into the outer bowl of Ninja CREAMi. 8. Install the "Creamerizer Paddle" onto the lid of outer bowl. 9. Then rotate the lid clockwise to lock. 10. Press "Power" button to turn on the unit. 11. Then press "GELATO" button. 12. When the program is completed, turn the outer bowl and release it from the machine. Transfer the gelato into serving bowls and serve immediately.

Pecan Gelato

Prep time: 10 minutes | Cook time: 3 minutes | Serves 4
4 large egg yolks
5 tablespoons granulated sugar
1 tablespoon light corn syrup
1 cup heavy cream
⅓ cup whole milk
1 teaspoon butter flavor extract
⅓ cup pecans, chopped

1. In a small saucepan, add the egg yolks, sugar and corn syrup and beat until well combined. 2. Add the heavy cream, milk and butter flavor extract and beat until well combined. 3. Place the saucepan over medium heat and cook for about 2-3 minutes, stirring continuously. 4. Remove from the heat and through a fine-mesh strainer, strain the mixture into an empty Ninja CREAMi pint container. 5. Place the container into an ice bath to cool. 6. After cooling, cover the container with the storage lid and freeze for 24 hours. 7. After 24 hours, remove the lid from container and arrange into the outer bowl of Ninja CREAMi. 8. Install the "Creamerizer Paddle" onto the lid of outer bowl. 9. Then rotate the lid clockwise to lock. 10. Press "Power" button to turn on the unit. 11. Then press "GELATO" button. 12. When the program is completed, with a spoon, create a 1½-inch wide hole in the center that reaches the bottom of the pint container. 13. Add the pecans into the hole and press "MIX-IN" button. 14. When the program is completed, turn the outer bowl and release it from the machine. 15. Transfer the gelato into serving bowls and serve immediately.

Cantaloupe Sorbet

Prep time: 5 minutes | Cook time: 10 minutes | Serves 4
3 cups cantaloupe pieces
⅓ cup water
⅓ cup organic sugar
1 tablespoon freshly squeezed lemon juice

1. Combine the cantaloupe, water, sugar, and lemon juice in a blender. Blend on high until smooth. 2. Pour the base into a clean CREAMi Pint. Place the storage lid on the container and freeze for 24 hours. 3. Remove the pint from the freezer and take off the lid. Place the pint in the outer bowl of your Ninja CREAMi, install the Creamerizer Paddle in the outer bowl lid, and lock the lid assembly onto the outer

bowl. Place the bowl assembly on the motor base, and twist the handle to the right to raise the platform and lock it in place. Select the Sorbet function. 4. Once the machine has finished processing, remove the sorbet from the pint. Serve immediately.

Vanilla Bean Gelato

Prep time: 5 minutes | Cook time: 3 minutes | Serves 4
4 large egg yolks
1 tablespoon light corn syrup
¼ cup plus 1 tablespoon granulated sugar
⅓ cup whole milk
1 cup heavy (whipping) cream
1 whole vanilla bean, split in half lengthwise and scraped

1. Fill a large bowl with ice water and set it aside. 2. In a small saucepan, whisk together the egg yolks, corn syrup, and sugar until everything is fully combined and the sugar is dissolved. Do not do this over heat. 3. Whisk in the milk, heavy cream, and vanilla bean scrapings (discard the pod). 4. Place the pan over medium heat. Cook, stirring constantly with a rubber spatula, until the temperature reaches 165°F to 175°F on an instant-read thermometer. 5. Remove the pan from the heat and pour the base through a fine-mesh strainer into a clean CREAMi Pint. Carefully place the container in the prepared ice water bath, making sure the water doesn't spill into the base. 6. Once the base has cooled, place the storage lid on the pint and freeze for 24 hours. 7. Remove the pint from the freezer and take off the lid. Place the pint in the outer bowl of your Ninja CREAMi, install the Creamerizer Paddle in the outer bowl lid, and lock the lid assembly onto the outer bowl. Place the bowl assembly on the motor base, and twist the handle to the right to raise the platform and lock it in place. Select the Gelato function. 8. Once the machine has finished processing, remove the gelato from the pint. Serve immediately with desired toppings.

Cherry Gelato

Prep time: 6 minutes | Cook time: 3 minutes | Serves 4
4 large egg yolks
1 tablespoon light corn syrup
5 tablespoons granulated sugar
1 cup heavy cream
⅓ cup whole milk
1 teaspoon almond extract
1 cup frozen black cherries, pitted and quartered

1. In a small saucepan, add the egg yolks, sugar and corn syrup and beat until well combined. 2. Add the heavy cream, milk and almond extract and beat until well combined. 3. Place the saucepan over medium heat and cook for about 2-3 minutes, stirring continuously. 4. Remove from the heat and through a fine-mesh strainer, strain the mixture into an empty Ninja CREAMi pint container. 5. Place the container into an ice bath to cool. 6. After cooling, cover the container with the storage lid and freeze for 24 hours. 7. After 24 hours, remove the lid from container and arrange into the outer bowl of Ninja CREAMi. 8. Install the "Creamerizer Paddle" onto the lid of outer bowl. 9. Then rotate the lid clockwise to lock. 10. Press "Power" button to turn on the unit. 11. Then press "GELATO" button. 12. When the program is completed, with a spoon, create a 1½-inch wide hole in the center that reaches the bottom of the pint container. 13. Add the cherries into the hole and press "MIX-IN" button. 14. When the program is completed, turn the outer bowl and release it from the machine. 15. Transfer the gelato into serving bowls and serve immediately.

Vanilla Gelato

Prep time: 5 minutes | Cook time: 3 minutes | Serves 4
4 large egg yolks
1 tablespoon light corn syrup
¼ cup plus 1 tablespoon granulated sugar
1 cup heavy cream
⅓ cup whole milk
1 whole vanilla bean, split in half lengthwise and scraped

1. In a small saucepan, add the egg yolks, corn syrup and sugar and beat until well combined. 2. Add the heavy cream, milk and vanilla bean and beat until well combined. 3. Place the saucepan over medium heat and cook for about 2-3 minutes,

stirring continuously. 4. Remove from the heat and through a fine-mesh strainer, strain the mixture into an empty Ninja CREAMi pint container. 5. Place the container into an ice bath to cool. 6. After cooling, cover the container with the storage lid and freeze for 24 hours. 7. After 24 hours, remove the lid from container and arrange into the outer bowl of Ninja CREAMi. 8. Install the "Creamerizer Paddle" onto the lid of outer bowl. 9. Then rotate the lid clockwise to lock. 10. Press "Power" button to turn on the unit. 11. Then press "GELATO" button. 12. When the program is completed, turn the outer bowl and release it from the machine. 13. Transfer the gelato into serving bowls and serve immediately.

White Chocolate–raspberry Gelato

Prep time: 10 minutes | Cook time: 10 minutes | Serves 4
1 cup whole milk, divided
1 tablespoon, plus ¼ cup cornstarch
½ cup heavy (whipping) cream
1 teaspoon vanilla extract
⅓ cup, plus ¾ cup granulated sugar
½ cup raspberries
4 tablespoons water, divided
¼ cup white chocolate chips

1. Fill a large bowl with ice water and set it aside. 2. In a small bowl, mix together ⅓ cup of milk and 1 tablespoon of cornstarch; set aside. 3. In a small saucepan, combine the remaining ⅔ cup of milk, the heavy cream, vanilla, and ⅓ cup of sugar. Whisk thoroughly to combine. 4. Place the pan over medium-high heat and bring the mixture to a simmer for about 4 minutes. Whisk in the cornstarch slurry and continue whisking constantly for about 1 minute. 5. Remove the pan from the heat and pour the base through a fine-mesh strainer into a clean CREAMi Pint. Carefully place the container in the prepared ice water bath, making sure the water doesn't spill into the base. 6. While the base chills, place the raspberries, remaining ¾ cup of sugar, and 2 tablespoons of water in a small saucepan. Place the pan over medium heat. Cook, stirring constantly, for about 5 minutes, until the mixture is bubbling and the raspberries have broken down. 7. In a small bowl, whisk together the remaining 2 tablespoons of water and ¼ cup of cornstarch. Pour this mixture into the raspberry liquid. Continue to cook, stirring until the mixture has thickened, about 1 minute. Pour the raspberry mixture into a clean container, then carefully place the container in the ice water bath, making sure the water doesn't spill inside the container. 8. Once the base and raspberry mixtures are cold, carefully fold the raspberry mixture into the gelato base. Pour this mixture back into the CREAMi Pint, place the storage lid on the container, and freeze for 24 hours. 9. Remove the

pint from the freezer and take off the lid. Place the pint in the outer bowl of your Ninja CREAMi, install the Creamerizer Paddle in the outer bowl lid, and lock the lid assembly onto the outer bowl. Place the bowl assembly on the motor base, and twist the handle to the right to raise the platform and lock it in place. Select the Gelato function. 10. Once the machine has finished processing, remove the lid from the pint. With a spoon, create a 1½-inch-wide hole that reaches the bottom of the pint. During this process, it is okay if your treat reaches above the Max Fill line. Add the white chocolate chips to the hole in the pint, replace the lid, and select the Mix-In function. 11. Once the machine has finished processing, remove the gelato from the pint. Serve immediately with desired toppings.

Apple Cider Sorbet

Prep time: 5 minutes | Cook time: 3 minutes | Serves 4
1 cup apple cider
1 cup applesauce
2 tablespoons organic sugar

1. In a large bowl, whisk together the apple cider, applesauce, and sugar until the sugar is dissolved. 2. Pour the base into a clean CREAMi Pint. Place the storage lid on the container and freeze for 24 hours. 3. Remove the pint from the freezer and take off the lid. Place the pint in the outer bowl of your Ninja CREAMi, install the Creamerizer Paddle in the outer bowl lid, and lock the lid assembly onto the outer bowl. Place the bowl assembly on the motor base, and twist the handle to the right to raise the platform and lock it in place. Select the Sorbet function. 4. Once the machine has finished processing, remove the sorbet from the pint. Serve immediately.

Carrot Gelato

Prep time: 5 minutes | Cook time: 3 minutes | Serves 4

3 large egg yolks
⅓ cup coconut sugar
1 tablespoon brown rice syrup
½ cup heavy cream
1 cup unsweetened almond milk
½ cup carrot puree

½ teaspoon ground cinnamon
¼ teaspoon ground nutmeg
¼ teaspoon ground ginger
¼ teaspoon ground cloves
¾ teaspoon vanilla extract

1. In a small saucepan, add the egg yolks, coconut sugar and brown rice syrup and beat until well combined. 2. Add the heavy cream, almond milk, carrot puree and spices and beat until well combined. 3. Place the saucepan over medium heat and

cook for about 2-3 minutes, stirring continuously. 4. Remove from the heat and stir in the vanilla extract. 5. Through a fine-mesh strainer, strain the mixture into an empty Ninja CREAMi pint container. 6. Place the container into an ice bath to cool. 7. After cooling, cover the container with the storage lid and freeze for 24 hours. 8. After 24 hours, remove the lid from container and arrange into the outer bowl of Ninja CREAMi. 9. Install the "Creamerizer Paddle" onto the lid of outer bowl. 10. Then rotate the lid clockwise to lock. 11. Press "Power" button to turn on the unit. 12. Then press "GELATO" button. 13. When the program is completed, turn the outer bowl and release it from the machine. 14. Transfer the gelato into serving bowls and serve immediately.

Strawberry Cheesecake Gelato

Prep time: 5 minutes | Cook time: 8 minutes | Serves 4
4 large egg yolks
3 tablespoons granulated sugar
1 cup whole milk
⅓ cup heavy (whipping) cream
¼ cup cream cheese, at room temperature
1 teaspoon vanilla extract
3 tablespoons strawberry jam
¼ cup graham cracker pieces

1. Fill a large bowl with ice water and set it aside. 2. In a small saucepan, whisk together the egg yolks and sugar until the mixture is smooth and the sugar is dissolved. Do not do this over heat. 3. Whisk in the milk, heavy cream, cream cheese, vanilla, and strawberry jam. 4. Place the pan over medium heat. Cook, stirring constantly with a rubber spatula, until the temperature reaches 165°F to 175°F on an instant-read thermometer. 5. Remove the pan from the heat and pour the base through a fine-mesh strainer into a clean CREAMi Pint. Carefully place the container in the prepared ice water bath, making sure the water doesn't spill into the base. 6. Once the base has cooled, place the storage lid on the pint and freeze for 24 hours. 7. Remove the pint from the freezer and take off the lid. Place the pint in the outer bowl of your Ninja CREAMi, install the Creamerizer Paddle in the outer bowl lid, and lock the lid assembly onto the outer bowl. Place the bowl assembly on the motor base, and twist the handle to the right to raise the platform and lock it in place. Select the Gelato function. 8. Once the machine has finished processing, remove the lid from the pint container. With a spoon, create a 1½-inch-wide hole that reaches the bottom of the pint. During this process, it is okay if your treat reaches above the Max Fill line. Add the graham cracker pieces to the hole in the pint, replace the lid, and select the Mix-In function. 9. Once the

machine has finished processing, remove the gelato from the pint. Serve immediately.

Banana & Squash Cookie Gelato

Prep time: 5 minutes | Cook time: 3 minutes | Serves 4

4 large egg yolks
1 cup heavy cream
⅓ cup granulated sugar
½ of banana, peeled and sliced
½ cup frozen butternut squash, chopped
1 box instant vanilla pudding mix
6 vanilla wafer cookies, crumbled

1. In a small saucepan, add the egg yolks, heavy cream and sugar and beat until well combined. 2. Place the saucepan over medium heat and cook for about 2-3 minutes, stirring continuously. 3. Remove from the heat and through a fine-mesh strainer, strain the mixture into an empty Ninja CREAMi pint container. 4. Place the container into an ice bath to cool. 5. After cooling, add in the banana, squash and pudding until well combined. 6. Cover the container with the storage lid and freeze for 24 hours. 7. After 24 hours, remove the lid from container and arrange into the outer bowl of Ninja CREAMi. 8. Install the "Creamerizer Paddle" onto the lid of outer bowl. 9. Then rotate the lid clockwise to lock. 10. Press "Power" button to turn on the unit. 11. Then press "GELATO" button. 12. When the program is completed, with a spoon, create a 1½-inch wide hole in the center that reaches the bottom of the pint container. 13. Add the wafer cookies into the hole and press "MIX-IN" button. 14. When the program is completed, turn the outer bowl and release it from the machine. 15. Transfer the gelato into serving bowls and serve immediately.

Chocolate Cauliflower Gelato

Prep time: 15 minutes | Cook time: 3 minutes | Serves 4

1 cup whole milk
½ cup heavy cream
⅓ cup sugar
2 tablespoons cocoa powder
½ cup frozen cauliflower rice
¼ teaspoon almond extract
Pinch of salt
½ cup dark chocolate, chopped

1. In a small saucepan, add all ingredients except for chopped chocolate and beat until well combined. 2. Place the saucepan over medium heat and cook for about 2-3 minutes, stirring continuously. 3. Remove from the heat and transfer the mixture into an empty Ninja CREAMi pint container. 4. Place the container into an ice bath to cool. 5. After cooling, cover the container with the storage lid and freeze for 24 hours. 6. After 24 hours, remove the lid from container and arrange into the outer bowl of Ninja CREAMi. 7. Install the "Creamerizer Paddle" onto the lid of outer bowl. 8. Then rotate the lid clockwise to lock. 9. Press "Power" button to turn on the unit. 10. Then press "GELATO" button. 11. When the program is completed, with a spoon, create a 1½-inch wide hole in the center that reaches the bottom of the pint container. 12. Add the chopped chocolate into the hole and press "MIX-IN" button. 13. When the program is completed, turn the outer bowl and release it from the machine. 14. Transfer the gelato into serving bowls and serve immediately.

Red Velvet Gelato

Prep time: 5 minutes | Cook time: 3 minutes | Serves 4

4 large egg yolks

¼ cup granulated sugar

2 tablespoons unsweetened cocoa powder

1 cup whole milk

⅓ cup heavy (whipping) cream

¼ cup cream cheese, at room temperature

1 teaspoon vanilla extract

1 teaspoon red food coloring

1. Fill a large bowl with ice water and set it aside. 2. In a small saucepan, whisk together the egg yolks, sugar, and cocoa powder until everything is fully combined and the sugar is dissolved. Do not do this over heat. 3. Whisk in the milk, heavy cream, cream cheese, vanilla, and food coloring. 4. Place the pan over medium heat. Cook, stirring constantly with a rubber spatula, until the temperature reaches 165°F to 175°F on an instant-read thermometer. 5. Remove the pan from the heat and pour the base through a fine-mesh strainer into a clean CREAMi Pint. Carefully place the container in the prepared ice water bath, making sure the water doesn't spill into the base. 6. Once the base has cooled, place the storage lid on the pint and freeze for 24 hours. 7. Remove the pint from the freezer and take off the lid. Place the pint in the outer bowl of your Ninja CREAMi, install the Creamerizer Paddle in the outer bowl lid, and lock the lid assembly onto the outer bowl. Place the bowl assembly on the motor base, and twist the handle to the right to raise the platform and lock it in place. Select the Gelato function. 8. Once the machine has finished processing, remove the gelato from the pint. Serve immediately.

Squash Gelato

Prep time: 5 minutes | Cook time: 5 minutes | Serves 4
1¾ cups milk
½ cup cooked butternut squash
¼ cup granulated sugar
½ teaspoon ground cinnamon
¼ teaspoon ground allspice
Pinch of salt

1. In a small saucepan, add all ingredients and beat until well combined. 2. Place the saucepan over medium heat and cook for about 5 minutes, stirring continuously. 3. Remove from the heat and transfer the mixture into an empty Ninja CREAMi pint container. 4. Place the container into an ice bath to cool. 5. After cooling, cover the container with the storage lid and freeze for 24 hours. 6. After 24 hours, remove the lid from container and arrange into the outer bowl of Ninja CREAMi. 7. Install the "Creamerizer Paddle" onto the lid of outer bowl. 8. Then rotate the lid clockwise to lock. 9. Press "Power" button to turn on the unit. 10. Then press "GELATO" button. 11. When the program is completed, turn the outer bowl and release it from the machine. 12. Transfer the gelato into serving bowls and serve immediately.

Marshmallow Gelato

Prep time: 20 minutes | Cook time: 5 minutes | Serves 4
1 cup whole milk
½ cup heavy cream
¼ cup sugar
3 egg yolk
Pinch of sea salt
¼ cup mini marshmallows

1. Preheat the oven to broiler. Lightly grease a baking sheet. 2. Arrange the marshmallows onto the prepared baking sheet in a single layer. 3. Broil for about 5 minutes, flipping once halfway through. 4. Meanwhile, in a small saucepan, add the milk, heavy cream, sugar, egg yolks and a pinch of salt and beat until well combined. 5. Place the saucepan over medium heat and cook for about 1 minute, stirring continuously. 6. Remove from the heat and stir in half of the marshmallows. 7. Transfer the mixture into an empty Ninja CREAMi pint container. 8. Place the container into an ice bath to cool. 9. After cooling, cover the

container with the storage lid and freeze for 24 hours. 10. Reserve the remaining marshmallows into the freezer. 11. After 24 hours, remove the lid from container and arrange into the outer bowl of Ninja CREAMi. 12. Install the "Creamerizer Paddle" onto the lid of outer bowl. 13. Then rotate the lid clockwise to lock. 14. Press "Power" button to turn on the unit. 15. Then press "GELATO" button. 16. When the program is completed, with a spoon, create a 1½-inch wide hole in the center that reaches the bottom of the pint container. 17. Add the reserved frozen marshmallows into the hole and press "MIX-IN" button. 18. When the program is completed, turn the outer bowl and release it from the machine. 19. Transfer the gelato into serving bowls and serve immediately.

Chocolate Hazelnut Gelato

Prep time: 5 minutes | Cook time: 3 minutes | Serves 4
3 large egg yolks
⅓ cup hazelnut spread
¼ cup granulated sugar
2 teaspoons cocoa powder
1 tablespoon light corn syrup
1 cup whole milk
½ cup heavy cream
1 teaspoon vanilla extract

1. In a small saucepan, add the egg yolks, hazelnut spread, sugar, cocoa powder and corn syrup and beat until well combined. 2. Add the milk, heavy cream and vanilla extract and beat until well combined. 3. Place the saucepan over medium heat and cook for about 2-3 minutes, stirring continuously. 4. Remove from the heat and through a fine-mesh strainer, strain the mixture into an empty Ninja CREAMi pint container. 5. Place the container into an ice bath to cool. 6. After cooling, cover the container with the storage lid and freeze for 24 hours. 7. After 24 hours, remove the lid from container and arrange into the outer bowl of Ninja CREAMi. 8. Install the "Creamerizer Paddle" onto the lid of outer bowl. 9. Then rotate the lid clockwise to lock. 10. Press "Power" button to turn on the unit. 11. Then press "GELATO" button. 12. When the program is completed, turn the outer bowl and release it from the machine. 13. Transfer the gelato into serving bowls and serve immediately.

Chapter 6 Ice Cream Recipes

Chapter 6 Ice Cream Recipes

Chocolate & Spinach Ice Cream

Prep time: 5 minutes | Cook time: 5 minutes | Serves 2

½ cup frozen spinach, thawed and squeezed dry
1 cup whole milk
½ cup granulated sugar
1 teaspoon mint extract
3-5 drops green food coloring
⅓ cup heavy cream
¼ cup chocolate chunks, chopped
¼ cup brownie, cut into 1-inch pieces

1. In a high-speed blender, add the spinach, milk, sugar, mint extract and food coloring and pulse until mixture smooth. 2. Transfer the mixture into an empty Ninja CREAMi pint container. 3. Add the heavy cream and stir until well combined. 4. Cover the container with the storage lid and freeze for 24 hours. 5. After 24 hours, remove the lid from container and arrange into the outer bowl of Ninja CREAMi. 6. Install the "Creamerizer Paddle" onto the lid of outer bowl 7. Then rotate the lid clockwise to lock. 8. Press "Power" button to turn on the unit. 9. Then press "ICE CREAM" button. 10. When the program is completed, with a spoon, create a 1½-inch wide hole in the center that reaches the bottom of the pint container. 11. Add the chocolate chunks and brownie pieces into the hole and press "MIX-IN" button. 12. When the program is completed, turn the outer bowl and release it from the machine. 13. Transfer the ice cream into serving bowls and serve immediately.

Mango Ice Cream

Prep time: 5 minutes | Cook time: 5 minutes | Serves 1
1 mango (medium-sized, cut into quarters)
1 tablespoon cream cheese (room temperature)
¼ cup sugar
¾ cup heavy whipping cream
1 cup milk

1. Combine the cream cheese, sugar in a mixing bowl. Using a whisk, mix together until all ingredients are thoroughly combined, and the sugar starts to dissolve. 2. Add in the heavy whipping cream and milk. Whisk until all ingredients have combined well. 3. Pour mixture into an empty ninja CREAMi Pint container. Freeze for 24 hours after adding the mango to the Pint, ensuring you don't go over the maximum fill line. 4. Take the Pint out of the freezer after 24 hours. Take off the cover. 5. Place the Ninja CREAMi Pint into the outer bowl. Place the outer bowl with the Pint in it into the ninja CREAMi machine and turn until the outer bowl locks into place. Push the ICE CREAM button. During the ICE CREAM function, the ice cream will mix and become very creamy. 11. Once the ICE CREAM function has ended, turn the outer bowl and release it from the ninja CREAMi machine.

Cherry-chocolate Chunk Ice Cream

Prep time: 5 minutes | Cook time: 10 minutes | Serves 4
1 packet frozen sweet cherries
¾ cup heavy cream
1 can sweetened condensed milk
½ cup milk
1 teaspoon vanilla extract
1 bar semisweet baking chocolate, broken into small chunks

1. Combine the heavy cream, sweetened condensed milk, milk, and vanilla extract in a mixing bowl. 2. Pour the ice cream mixture into an empty ninja CREAMi Pint container, add the chopped cherries and chocolate chunks, and freeze for 24 hours. 3. After 24 hours, remove the Pint from the freezer. Remove the lid. 4. Place the Ninja CREAMi Pint into the outer bowl. Place the outer bowl with the Pint in it into the ninja CREAMi machine and turn until the outer bowl locks into place. Push the ICE CREAM button. 5. Once the ICE CREAM function has ended, turn the outer bowl and release it from the ninja CREAMi machine.

Pear Ice Cream

Prep time: 5 minutes | Cook time: 15 minutes | Serves 4
3 medium ripe pears, peeled, cored and cut into 1-inch pieces
1 can full-fat unsweetened coconut milk
½ cup granulated sugar

1. In a medium saucepan, add all ingredients and stir to combine. 2. Place the saucepan over medium heat and bring to a boil. 3. Reduce the heat to low and simmer for about ten minutes or until liquid is reduced by half. 4. Remove from the heat and set aside to cool. 5. After cooling, transfer the mixture into a high-speed blender and pulse until smooth. 6. Transfer the mixture into an empty Ninja CREAMi pint container. 7. Cover the container with storage lid and freeze for 24 hours. 8. After 24 hours, remove the lid from container and arrange into the Outer Bowl of Ninja CREAMi. 9. Install the Creamerizer Paddle onto the lid of Outer Bowl. 10. Then rotate the lid clockwise to lock. 11. Press Power button to turn on the unit. 12. Then press Ice Cream button. 13. When the program is completed, turn the Outer Bowl and release it from the machine. 14. Transfer the ice cream into serving bowls and serve immediately.

Mocha Ice Cream

Prep time: 5 minutes | Cook time: 5 minutes | Serves 4
½ cup mocha cappuccino mix
1¾ cups coconut cream
3 tablespoons agave nectar

1. In a bowl, add all ingredients and beat until well combined. 2. Transfer the mixture into an empty Ninja CREAMi pint container. 3. Cover the container with storage lid and freeze for 24 hours. 4. After 24 hours, remove the lid from container and arrange into the Outer Bowl of Ninja CREAMi. 5. Install the Creamerizer Paddle onto the lid of Outer Bowl. 6. Then rotate the lid clockwise to lock. 7. Press Power button to turn on the unit. 8. Then press Ice Cream button. 9. When the program is completed, turn the Outer Bowl and release it from the machine. 10. Transfer the ice cream into serving bowls and serve immediately.

Fruity Extract Ice Cream

Prep time: 5 minutes | Cook time: 5 minutes | Serves 4
1 cup whole milk
¾ cup heavy cream
2 tablespoons monk fruit sweetener with Erythritol
2 tablespoons agave nectar
½ teaspoon raspberry extract
½ teaspoon vanilla extract
¼ teaspoon lemon extract
5-6 drops blue food coloring

1. In a bowl, add all ingredients and eat until well combined. 2. Transfer the mixture into an empty Ninja CREAMi pint container. 3. Cover the container with storage lid and freeze for 24 hours. 4. After 24 hours, remove the lid from container and arrange into the Outer Bowl of Ninja CREAMi. 5. Install the Creamerizer Paddle onto the lid of outer bowl. 6. Then rotate the lid clockwise to lock. 7. Press Power button to turn on the unit. 8. Then press Ice Cream button. 9. When the program is completed, turn the Outer Bowl and release it from the machine. 10. Transfer the ice cream into serving bowls and serve immediately.

Fruity Carrot Ice Cream

Prep time: 5 minutes | Cook time: 5 minutes | Serves 4
¾ cup heavy cream
½ cup milk
⅓ cup orange juice
¾ cup sugar
¼ cup frozen carrots
¼ cup pineapple chunks

1. In a bowl, add the heavy cream, milk, orange juice and sugar and beat until well combined. 2. In an empty Ninja CREAMi pint container, place the carrots and pineapple chunks and top with milk mixture. 3. Cover the container with the storage lid and freeze for 24 hours. 4. After 24 hours, remove the lid from container and arrange into the outer bowl of Ninja CREAMi. 5. Install the "Creamerizer Paddle" onto the lid of outer bowl. 6. Then rotate the lid clockwise to lock. 7. Press "Power" button to turn on the unit. 8. Then press "ICE CREAM" button. 9. When the program is completed, turn the outer bowl and release it from the machine. 10. Transfer the ice cream into serving bowls and serve immediately.

Creamy Caramel Macchiato Coffee Ice Cream

Prep time: 5 minutes | Cook time: 5 minutes | Serves 6
1 cup heavy whipping cream
½ cup sweetened condensed milk
¼ cup coffee-mate caramel macchiato flavored creamer (liquid creamer)
1 teaspoon instant coffee granules
Caramel syrup (for drizzling)

1. Combine all ingredients (except the syrup) in a big mixing bowl of a stand mixer or a large mixing dish. 2. Whip the heavy cream mixture with an electric mixer until firm peaks form (to prevent massive splattering, start at a slower speed, and as the cream thickens, increase the speed). Make sure the whip cream mixture isn't overmixed or "broken." 3. Pour the mixture into an empty ninja CREAMi Pint container and freeze for 24 hours. 4. After 24 hours, remove the Pint from the freezer. Remove the lid. 5. Place the Ninja CREAMi Pint into the outer bowl. Place the outer bowl with the Pint in it into the ninja CREAMi machine and turn until the outer bowl locks into place. Push the ICE CREAM button. 6. Once the ICE CREAM function has ended, turn the outer bowl and release it from the ninja CREAMi machine.

Super Lemon Ice Cream

Prep time: 5 minutes | Cook time: 20 minutes | Serves 5
1 cup heavy whipping cream
½ cup half-and-half cream
½ cup white sugar
1 tablespoon grated lemon zest
2 egg yolks
¼ cup fresh lemon juice

1. On low heat, whisk together the heavy cream, half-and-half cream, sugar, and lemon zest in a saucepan until the sugar is dissolved. 2. In a mixing dish, whisk together the egg yolks. 3. Stir in a few tablespoons of the cream mixture at a time into the eggs. This will assist in bringing the eggs up to temperature without them becoming scrambled. Return the egg mixture to the bowl with the cream mixture. 4. Pour the mixture into an empty ninja CREAMi Pint container, add lemon, and freeze for 24 hours. 5. After 24 hours, remove the Pint from the freezer. Remove the lid. 6. Place the Ninja CREAMi Pint into the outer bowl. Place the outer bowl with the Pint in it into the ninja CREAMi machine and turn until the outer bowl

locks into place. Push the ICE CREAM button. 7. Once the ICE CREAM function has ended, turn the outer bowl and release it from the ninja CREAMi machine.

French Vanilla Ice Cream

Prep time: 5 minutes | Cook time: 5 minutes | Serves 4
4 large egg yolks
1 tablespoon light corn syrup
¼ cup plus 1 tablespoon granulated sugar
⅓ cup whole milk
1 cup heavy (whipping) cream
1 teaspoon vanilla extract

1. Fill a large bowl with ice water and set it aside. 2. In a small saucepan, whisk together the egg yolks, corn syrup, and sugar until the mixture is fully combined and the sugar is dissolved. Do not do this over heat. 3. Whisk in the milk, heavy cream, and vanilla until combined. 4. Place the pan over medium heat. Cook, stirring constantly with a rubber spatula, until the temperature reaches 165°F to 175°F on an instant-read thermometer. 5. Remove the pan from the heat and pour the base through a fine-mesh strainer into a clean CREAMi Pint. Carefully place the container in the prepared ice water bath, making sure the water doesn't spill into the base. 6. Once the base has cooled, place the storage lid on the pint and freeze for 24 hours. 7. Remove the CREAMi Pint from the freezer and take off the lid. Place the pint in the outer bowl of your Ninja CREAMi, install the Creamerizer Paddle in the outer bowl lid, and lock the lid assembly onto the outer bowl. Place the bowl assembly on the motor base, and twist the handle to the right to raise the platform and lock it in place. Select the Ice Cream function. 8. Once the machine has finished processing, remove the ice cream from the pint. Serve immediately.

Cinnamon Red Hot Ice Cream

Prep time: 5 minutes | Cook time: 10 minutes | Serves 5
2 cups heavy whipping cream, divided
1 egg yolk
1 cup half-and-half
½ cup Red Hot candies

1. In a mixing bowl, whisk together 1 cup of cream and the egg yolks until smooth. 2. In another large bowl, combine the half-and-half, 1 cup cream, and Red Hot candies. Whisk with a wooden spoon until the candies dissolve, about 5 to 10 minutes. 3. Pour the cream-egg mixture into the candy mixture and stir to incorporate. 4. Pour the mixture into an empty ninja CREAMi Pint container and freeze for 24 hours. 5. After 24 hours, remove the Pint from the freezer. Remove the lid. 6. Place the Ninja CREAMi Pint into the outer bowl. Place the outer bowl with the Pint in it into the ninja CREAMi machine and turn until the outer bowl locks into place. Push the ICE CREAM button. 7. Once the ICE CREAM function has ended, turn the outer bowl and release it from the ninja CREAMi machine.

Low-sugar Vanilla Ice Cream

Prep time: 5 minutes | Cook time: 5 minutes | Serves 4
1¾ cup fat-free half-and-half
¼ cup stevia cane sugar blend
1 teaspoon vanilla extract

1. In a medium bowl, whisk the half-and-half, sugar, and vanilla together until everything is combined and the sugar is dissolved. The mixture will be foamy. Let it sit for 5 minutes or until the foam subsides. 2. Pour the base into a clean CREAMi Pint. Place the storage lid on the container and freeze for 24 hours. 3. Remove the CREAMi Pint from the freezer and take off the lid. Place the pint in the outer bowl of your Ninja CREAMi, install the Creamerizer Paddle in the outer bowl lid, and lock the lid assembly onto the outer bowl. Place the bowl assembly on the motor base, and twist the handle to the right to raise the platform and lock it in place. Select the Lite Ice Cream function. 4. Once the machine has finished processing, remove the ice cream from the pint. Serve immediately.

Coconut Ice Cream

Prep time: 5 minutes | Cook time: 5 minutes | Serves 4
½ cup milk
1 can cream of coconut
¾ cup heavy cream
½ cup sweetened flaked coconut

1. In a food processor or blender, combine the milk and coconut cream and thoroughly mix. 2. Combine the heavy cream and flaked coconut in a mixing bowl, and then add to the milk-cream mixture. Combine well. 3. Pour the mixture into an empty ninja CREAMi Pint container and freeze for 24 hours. 4. After 24 hours, remove the Pint from the freezer. Remove the lid. 5. Place the Ninja CREAMi Pint into the outer bowl. Place the outer bowl with the Pint in it into the ninja CREAMi machine and turn until the outer bowl locks into place. Push the ICE CREAM button. 6. Once the ICE CREAM function has ended, turn the outer bowl and release it from the ninja CREAMi machine.

Lemon Ice Cream

Prep time: 5 minutes | Cook time: 5 minutes | Serves 4
1 can full-fat unsweetened coconut milk
½ cup granulated sugar
1 teaspoon vanilla extract
1 teaspoon lemon extract

1. In a bowl, add the coconut milk and beat until smooth. 2. Add the remaining ingredients and beat until sugar is dissolved. 3. Transfer the mixture into an empty Ninja CREAMi pint container. 4. Cover the container with storage lid and freeze for 24 hours. 5. After 24 hours, remove the lid from container and arrange into the Outer Bowl of Ninja CREAMi. 6. Install the Creamerizer Paddle onto the lid of Outer Bowl. 7. Then rotate the lid clockwise to lock. 8. Press Power button to turn on the unit. 9. Then press Ice Cream button. 10. When the program is completed, turn the Outer Bowl and release it from the machine. 11. Transfer the ice cream into serving bowls and serve immediately.

Earl Grey Tea Ice Cream

Prep time: 5 minutes | Cook time: 25 minutes | Serves 4
1 cup heavy cream
1 cup whole milk
5 tablespoons monk fruit sweetener
3 Earl Grey tea bags

1. In a medium saucepan, add cream and milk and stir to combine. 2. Place saucepan over medium heat and cook until for bout two-three minutes or until steam is rising. 3. Stir in the monk fruit sweetener and reduce the heat to very low. 4. Add teabags and cover the saucepan for about 20 minutes. 5. Discard the tea bags and remove saucepan from heat. 6. Transfer the mixture into an empty Ninja CREAMi pint container and place into an ice bath to cool. 7. After cooling, cover the container with storage lid and freeze for 24 hours. 8. After 24 hours, remove the lid from container and arrange into the Outer Bowl of Ninja CREAMi. 9. Install the Creamerizer Paddle onto the lid of Outer Bowl. 10. Then rotate the lid clockwise to lock. 11. Press Power button to turn on the unit. 12. Then press Ice Cream button. 13. When the program is completed, turn the Outer Bowl and release it from the machine. 14. Transfer the ice cream into serving bowls and serve immediately.

Kale'd By Chocolate Ice Cream

Prep time: 5 minutes | Cook time: 5 minutes | Serves 4
1 cup frozen kale
1 tablespoon cream cheese, at room temperature
⅓ cup granulated sugar
3 tablespoons dark unsweetened cocoa powder
¾ cup whole milk
¾ cup heavy (whipping) cream

1. Combine the frozen kale, cream cheese, sugar, cocoa powder, and milk in a blender. Blend on high until smooth. 2. Pour the base into a clean CREAMi Pint. Whisk in the heavy cream until combined. Place the storage lid on the container and freeze for 24 hours. 3. Remove the CREAMi Pint from the freezer and take off the lid. Place the pint in the outer bowl of your Ninja CREAMi, install the Creamerizer Paddle in outer bowl lid, and lock the lid assembly onto the outer bowl. Place the bowl assembly on the motor base, and twist the handle to the right to raise the platform and lock it in place. Select the Ice Cream function. 4. Once the machine has finished processing, remove the ice cream from the pint. Serve

immediately with desired toppings.

Raspberry White Truffle Ice Cream

Prep time: 5 minutes | Cook time: 5 minutes | Serves 1
Ice cream base:
1 tablespoon cream cheese (room temperature)
⅓ cup sugar
1 tablespoon raspberry preserves
¾ cup heavy whipping cream
1 cup milk
¼ cup raspberries (cut in half)
Mix-ins:(optional)
¼ cup raspberries (cut in half)
3 white chocolate truffles (cut in quarters)

1. In a mixing dish, combine the cream cheese, sugar, and raspberry preserves. Using a whisk, blend all ingredients until they are thoroughly mixed and the sugar begins to dissolve. 2. Combine the heavy whipping cream and milk in a mixing bowl. Whisk until all of the ingredients are thoroughly blended. Because the raspberry preserves mixture is fairly thick, this may take a minute or two. 3. Half of the raspberries, cut in half, should be added. Depending on the size, this should yield 6 to 8 raspberries. 4. Once all ingredients have been added (except the mix-ins), pour into an empty ninja CREAMi Pint container and freeze for 24 hours. 5. After 24 hours, remove the Pint from the freezer. Remove the lid. 6. Place the Ninja CREAMi Pint into the outer bowl. Place the outer bowl with the Pint in it into the ninja CREAMi machine and turn until the outer bowl locks into place. Push the ICE CREAM button. During the ICE CREAM function, the ice cream will mix together and become very creamy. 7. Once the ICE CREAM function has ended, turn the outer bowl and release it from the ninja CREAMi machine. 8. Make a hole in the center of the ice cream with a spoon that runs from top to bottom. The mix-ins will be placed in this hole. Add the ¼ cup of raspberries and 3 white chocolate truffles to the mix. Make sure the raspberries are cut in half, and the truffles are sliced into quarters. Because these mix-ins will not be broken down into smaller bits during the mixing process, you'll want to make sure they're in little chunks. 9. Place the outer bowl with the Pint back into the ninja CREAMi machine and lock it into place. Choose the MIX-IN function. 10. Once the Ninja CREAMi completes the MIX-IN cycle, remove the outer bowl from the machine. 11. Your ice cream is ready to eat! Enjoy!

Coconut-vanilla Ice Cream

Prep time: 5 minutes | Cook time: 5 minutes | Serves 4
1 can full-fat unsweetened coconut milk
½ cup organic sugar
1 teaspoon vanilla extract

1. In a large bowl, whisk together the coconut milk, sugar, and vanilla until everything is incorporated and the sugar is dissolved. 2. Pour the base into a clean CREAMi Pint. Place the storage lid on the container and freeze for 24 hours. 3. Remove the CREAMi Pint from the freezer and take off the lid. Place the pint in the outer bowl of your Ninja CREAMi, install the Creamerizer Paddle in the outer bowl lid, and lock the lid assembly onto the outer bowl. Place the bowl assembly on the motor base, and twist the handle to the right to raise the platform and lock it in place. Select the Ice Cream function. 4. Once the machine has finished processing, remove the ice cream from the pint. Serve immediately with desired toppings.

Strawberry Ice Cream

Prep time: 5 minutes | Cook time: 5 minutes | Serves 4
¼ cup sugar
1 tablespoon cream cheese, softened
1 teaspoon vanilla bean paste
1 cup milk
¾ cup heavy whipping cream
6 medium fresh strawberries, hulled and quartered

1. In a bowl, add the sugar, cream cheese, vanilla bean paste and with a wire whisk, mix until well combined. 2. Add in the milk and heavy whipping cream and beat until well combined. 3. Transfer the mixture into an empty Ninja CREAMi pint container. 4. Add the strawberry pieces and stir to combine. 5. Cover the container with storage lid and freeze for 24 hours. 6. After 24 hours, remove the lid from container and arrange into the Outer Bowl of Ninja CREAMi. 7. Install the Creamerizer Paddle onto the lid of Outer Bowl. 8. Then rotate the lid clockwise to lock. 9. Press Power button to turn on the unit. 10. Then press Ice Cream button. 11. When the program is completed, turn the Outer Bowl and release it from the machine. 12. Transfer the ice cream into serving bowls and serve immediately.

Pumpkin Gingersnap Ice Cream

Prep time: 5 minutes | Cook time: 15 minutes | Serves 4

1 cup heavy whipping cream
½ tablespoon vanilla extract
½ teaspoon ground cinnamon
½ teaspoon ground ginger
½ cup solid-pack pumpkin
1 can Eagle Brand sweetened condensed milk
½ cup crushed gingersnap cookies

1. In a large mixing bowl, beat the heavy whipping cream, vanilla extract, cinnamon, and ginger with an electric mixer on medium speed until stiff peaks form. 2. Combine the pumpkin and sweetened condensed milk in a mixing bowl. 3. Add the crushed gingersnap cookies to the pumpkin mixture and stir well. 4. Pour the mixture into an empty ninja CREAMi Pint container and freeze for 24 hours. 5. After 24 hours, remove the Pint from the freezer. Remove the lid. 6. Place the Ninja CREAMi Pint into the outer bowl. Place the outer bowl with the Pint in it into the ninja CREAMi machine and turn until the outer bowl locks into place. Push the ICE CREAM button. 7. Once the ICE CREAM function has ended, turn the outer bowl and release it from the ninja CREAMi machine.

Conclusion

From my experience of using the Ninja CREAMi ice cream maker I can say that it is great for easily preparing healthy ice cream, sorbet, and frozen yoghurt at home. It takes some trial and error to figure out which recipes you prefer, but once you get it, you can make your ice cream at home with minimal mess, and it is wonderful! You may make as many different flavours as you want in a single day of ice cream within 3 minutes, as long as you remember to mix and freeze them the day before. Now its your turn to try this appliance yourself using our recipe collection and see how well it benefits you!

Appendix 1 Measurement Conversion Chart

MEASUREMENT CONVERSION CHART

VOLUME EQUIVALENTS(DRY)

US STANDARD	METRIC (APPROXIMATE)
1/8 teaspoon	0.5 mL
1/4 teaspoon	1 mL
1/2 teaspoon	2 mL
3/4 teaspoon	4 mL
1 teaspoon	5 mL
1 tablespoon	15 mL
1/4 cup	59 mL
1/2 cup	118 mL
3/4 cup	177 mL
1 cup	235 mL
2 cups	475 mL
3 cups	700 mL
4 cups	1 L

VOLUME EQUIVALENTS(LIQUID)

US STANDARD	US STANDARD (OUNCES)	METRIC (APPROXIMATE)
2 tablespoons	1 fl.oz.	30 mL
1/4 cup	2 fl.oz.	60 mL
1/2 cup	4 fl.oz.	120 mL
1 cup	8 fl.oz.	240 mL
1 1/2 cup	12 fl.oz.	355 mL
2 cups or 1 pint	16 fl.oz.	475 mL
4 cups or 1 quart	32 fl.oz.	1 L
1 gallon	128 fl.oz.	4 L

TEMPERATURES EQUIVALENTS

FAHRENHEIT(F)	CELSIUS(C) (APPROXIMATE)
225 °F	107 °C
250 °F	120 °C
275 °F	135 °C
300 °F	150 °C
325 °F	160 °C
350 °F	180 °C
375 °F	190 °C
400 °F	205 °C
425 °F	220 °C
450 °F	235 °C
475 °F	245 °C
500 °F	260 °C

WEIGHT EQUIVALENTS

US STANDARD	METRIC (APPROXIMATE)
1 ounce	28 g
2 ounces	57 g
5 ounces	142 g
10 ounces	284 g
15 ounces	425 g
16 ounces (1 pound)	455 g
1.5 pounds	680 g
2 pounds	907 g

Printed in the USA
CPSIA information can be obtained
at www.ICGtesting.com
LVHW080955161023
761219LV00003B/16